C000143652

PHOTOGRAPHERS' BRITAIN

YORKSHIRE

YORKSHIRE
Without you there would be no pride

PHOTOGRAPHERS' BRITAIN

YORKSHIRE

MICHAEL J. STEAD

ALAN SUTTON

First published in the United Kingdom in 1991
Alan Sutton Publishing Ltd · Phoenix Mill · Far Thrupp · Stroud · Gloucestershire

First Published in the United States of America in 1991
Alan Sutton Publishing Inc. · Wolfeboro Falls · NH 03896–0848

Copyright © Michael J. Stead, 1991

All rights reserved. No part of this publication may be reproduced, stored in a retrieval system, or transmitted, in any form, or by any means, electronic, mechanical, photocopying, recording or otherwise, without the prior permission of the publishers and copyright holders.

British Library Cataloguing in Publication Data

Stead, Michael J.
Photographers' Britain, Yorkshire.
1. England. Photography
I. Title
779.994281

ISBN 0–86299–840–9

Library of Congress Cataloguing-in-Publication Data

Stead. Michael J.
Photographers' Britain: Yorkshire / Michael J. Stead.
p. cm.
ISBN 0–86299–840–9
1. Yorkshire (England) – Description and travel–Views. I. Title.
DA670.Y6S77 1991
942.8'1–dc20   91–15171
                                                                           CIP

Typeset in 10/11 Sabon
Typesetting and origination by
Alan Sutton Publishing Limited.
Printed in Great Britain by
The Bath Press, Avon.

INTRODUCTION

When I first received the telephone call inviting me to produce this book, I eagerly accepted, as my one ambition had been to produce a series of photographs which illustrated Yorkshire through my eyes – my Yorkshire. It was only after I signed the contract that I began to break out in cold sweats and realized that I had been struck yet again by 'Steadism' – whenever I open my mouth, I seem inevitably not only to put one foot in it, but the other too, along with any others which happen to be handy. Photographically it was no problem, but to write a text was certainly a different kettle of typewriter keys. This work is not intended to be, not should it be viewed as, a comprehensive guide to Yorkshire, though inevitably it does include many well-known locations. However, as an intimate view of the county, some others will have been excluded, but equally, some neglected nooks of its broad acres are here, which I hope will provide an illuminating and interesting insight. Each of the places illustrated has over the years in some way struck a chord in me. The criteria for inclusion was as wide as the county itself. Perhaps personal memories of, and enjoyment of, a particular location; anecdotes and legend which might give an insight into Yorkshire pride; history which may do a little to explain the tenacity of her people; anger at how certain elements of the human race are desecrating our heritage. It is a journey on which I invite you to come, to share a little of the county to which my heart belongs.

One further point of great importance. The boundaries of the journey are the real Yorkshire, North, East and West Ridings. Consequently, it includes those parts now called Cleveland and Humberside (the mere mention of them requires me to take carbolic soap and a scrubbing brush to my mouth), which though stolen from us by faceless Whitehall bureaucrats, always in the mind of the inhabitants remain part of us.

I would like to acknowledge all those people, who over the years have, often unwittingly, helped my pride in the county to grow, and have provided the material which eventually enabled me to put this together. My appreciation to Alan Sutton staff

WHITBY HARBOUR

'at 'Mill', especially Jaqueline, who performed the unenviable task of editing my meandering manuscript without too many tears – from me I mean. In particular I would like to thank my mother and father for all their support, and for enabling me to be Yorkshire by birth, and to take this opportunity to apologize to Dad especially, for not being good enough for him to realize every Yorkshire father's dream of having a son play cricket for the county.

MICHAEL J. STEAD
JUNE, 1991

North Yorkshire Moors

It is quite common for communities in parts of the Moors and Dales to be isolated during a severe winter. The snowfall need not necessarily be very great, for prevailing winds can easily collect what there is and whip it into deep drifts. It is so much a fact of life, that such occurrences rarely warrant national media headlines as such an event in other parts of the country would. The inhabitants having become accustomed to this hardship, they usually manage to continue their daily business successfully.

At such times, I find that photographically the landscape exudes a particular charm and peacefulness which contradicts the reality of the conditions. This is especially so in close-up, where intricate patterns are created by snow and ice, on wood, stone, and in water. The trouble is that my pursuance of such images regularly leads me into difficult tiring situations, whether I be in a vehicle or on foot.

On this occasion the approaching storm broke with such ferocity that it necessitated the abandonment of my vehicle. I was indeed fortunate that the first door I stumbled upon, as I trudged through the swirling snow in search of shelter, happened to lead into the local public house. Though now safe, both myself and other unfortunate stranded patrons were cursing our luck at the prospect of being stranded there overnight, when the sound of a snow-plough was heard outside. I pitied the driver, who having blazed a trail through the blocked road, was rewarded with greetings somewhat less praiseworthy than his determination and dedication to the task deserved!

GRAVESTONE, LEEDS

I like to wander round and explore graveyards. Not through any sense of the macabre you understand, I just find the amount of social history in them very exciting. Poignant and unusual headstones, resting places of the famous and eccentric, epitaphs of local inhabitants. There's intrigue in cemetery gravestones which often spurs me on to research in which unusual stories unfold. For instance, that of Old George, who epitomized cynical Yorkshire humour, and had his last laugh from just such a refuge. In the twilight of his years, he often propped up the bar of his country local, but his quiet drinking was regularly interrupted by the local hunt members, who regaled him with their tales of prowess and huntsmanship, all of which he knew generally to be exaggerated ego-boosters. Finally, unable to stand a mutual back-slapping he pointed out to them that they only looked so good because they tracked down a dumb animal which was then overwhelmed by sheer advantage of numbers; confronted by a moderately clever opponent they would easily be made to look the incompetents they were. As you can imagine, this remark went down like an EEC agricultural minister at a Farmers' Union dinner-dance! He was ridiculed, scorned, and taunted until forced to leave, but not before declaring that he would prove his point one day.

Sadly, within a month he died; and as the days passed, his prediction was forgotten. Until after the next hunt meeting that is. As the members congregated at the end of the day, the landlord remarked how drained and subdued they appeared. It transpired that it wasn't only them, but also their hounds and horses. It seemed that they had been chasing a distinctively-marked fox, which had led them a merry dance, toyed with them, and returned to bait them if its trail went cold, until through necessity the chase had been abandoned: the first time no kill had been made in the hunt's history! The mood of dejection dispersed when someone entered the bar claiming to have seen the fox go to ground in the churchyard. In anger at being made to look fools, they resolved to absolve their embarrassment by completing the task with bare hands, and rushed out to the lair. Imagine their consternation upon finding that the burrow went beneath Old George's newly-erected headstone.

FARNDALE

It's funny how the best-known folk tales are constantly repeated. I promised myself that I wouldn't join the bandwagon, but it just goes to show how promises can easily be broken! I couldn't help it because the story of Sarkless Kitty is intriguing, and anyway the alleged site of the story provided an exceptionally good photograph!

Kitty was found drowned and sarkless, or for the less prude absolutely starkers, by the swollen river the morning after a great storm. The local community suspected that she thought her lover had failed to turn up at their rendezvous because of an illicit liaison with another. This led them to believe that she had committed suicide, and thus she was not allowed to be buried in consecrated ground. In fact, the man in question had decided to do the decent thing and had travelled to the local town to purchase a wedding ring. He was caught in the same storm as he returned, and his body turned up further along the same river barely three hours later. There was nothing for the community to do but to relent and arrange for the bodies to be buried side by side. However, by this time Kitty's body had disappeared, and a further mystery ensued, which has never satisfactorily been explained. Perhaps a Quaker couple, taking pity on the soul of Kitty, interred her body with the coffin of their daughter who was buried that morning, and perhaps this was proved much later when the grave was discovered to have two sets of bones. But if this is the case, why does Kitty's troubled spirit still roam the river-crossing at times of foul weather? Is she searching for a peaceful resting place or the lost soul of her beloved?

North Yorkshire Moors

The Moors at times can be the most hostile and lonely of places, with scant signs of habitation, human or animal. Yet over the centuries they have still needed to be traversed, hence the quite intricate system of pathways dissecting them. Many were merely simple single tracks to enable tinkers, priests, funeral processions and the like to travel between the various hamlets in the vales or the coast. This one on Rosedale Moor seems to have become the victim of modern destructive vehicles, eroded by transport used to convey the shooting fraternity to their shooting butts, with the minimum of exertion or loss of precious killing time.

In days gone by it might have taken several days to trek across the wild terrain, and to assist the wayfarers, markers were provided to ensure their path was not lost. Many of these had curious names such as Lilla Cross, Fat Betty, and Ralph's Cross, some of which remain, along with tales about them. In particular, the latter had at its top a hollow into which wealthier travellers who had safely crossed the moor might place some small token of thanks, which any less fortunate passing that way could take to assist with accommodation or food on their journey. Sad then that this practical symbol of camaraderie, which has stood for centuries, should very recently have succumbed to vandalism.

The inhospitality, and unpredictability, of the Moors are well known. They can entice you out into their barren acres with hot sunshine, only to change viciously without warning into dangerous storm-ravaged plateaux. It is probably no surprise therefore to find that the inhabitants who suffered such conditions constantly were influenced by the eeriness of their surroundings. They relied heavily on witchcraft; indeed, just prior to this century, having heard such rumours, the *Times* despatched a correspondent to write a short filler article. Discovering the prevalence of such beliefs, he stayed a month, and produced a major series which shocked and scandalized the capital. How could such an area, seemingly still in the Dark Ages, exist not 300 miles from what the Victorians somewhat hypocritically believed was the centre of civilization? The legacy of this is that today there is perhaps nowhere in the British Isles with a greater concentration of legends and folklore concerning hobs, wizards, spellbinders and spectral manifestations.

GLAISDALE PACK BRIDGE

There are two other crossings in addition to this one now: to the left for lead combustible vehicles, to the right for the Iron Horse. Once, though, there were none, and any journey across meant fording the river – a very difficult feat at any time, and impossible if it was running high and fast. This played havoc with lines of communication and, in particular for a man called Ferris, the path of true love. On one occasion, when trying to see his lady-friend, he almost drowned, and it was then he vowed that as soon as he was rich enough he would ensure no other local lad would have to endure such hardships in pursuit of pleasure.

Many of the local community scoffed at the vow, as poor Ferris did not have two ha'pennies to rub together. Soon afterwards he disappeared altogether. Rumours as to his whereabouts were rife, some saying he had gone to the New World, and others to Australia. Wherever he did go, it was certainly a lucrative move, because when he returned, he had no shortage of the 'readies' with which to fulfil his vow to build a bridge. Did he desire merely to be a benefactor to the community where he had spent his childhood, or did he provide the bridge as a kind of moral symbol – to show how any barrier to love, no matter how great, is surmountable, provided that the love is pure? Sadly, we will never know, for while most of the facts of this story can be proven, that which cannot is whether his nuptial bliss was indeed with the lady who had first instigated the vow.

ROSEBERRY TOPPING

It looks a lot higher than it really is, because it has all on to touch the thousand foot mark! Part of the illusion is caused by it being detached from all the surrounding hills. It also bears a remarkable resemblance to the Matterhorn, but looks are the only similarity, and even they are cosmetic – Roseberry Topping was created by the hand of man and not nature. It began life as a symmetrical conical hill, but the realization that it contained both alum and jet soon had miners burrowing into it. The removal of these enriched seams low down on its side, inevitably led to subsidence and the collapse of about half of the hill.

From here, which an attached plaque suggests was a hunting lodge to enable the local lord of the manor and his cronies to take pot shots at airborne innocents in relative comfort, the hill looks quite a daunting prospect; however, the effort required to scale the summit by the easy approach is relatively small, and the view from the top is very rewarding. It affords exceptional views towards the Hambletons, the Cleveland plain towards Teesside and the sea. On a clear day the area of Captain Cook's boyhood stretches below you towards the Pennines. This was one of my first hill-climbs, and I still enjoy repeating the exercise, particularly as a way of returning to fitness before extended photographic walking trips over more rugged terrain.

An interesting, but sad story, as to how a nearby village received its name is attached to the hill. When young Prince Oswald of Northumbria was born, the considered opinion of the wise men of the court was that he would not reach a year old. His father the king, mindful of how these prophecies were often fulfilled, by fair means or foul, built a cell just below the summit which could easily be defended. But while the prince slept there one night, a fearful storm erupted. The heavens opened, and such was the volume of rain that it placed a tremendous strain on the natural drainage system. This caused a hidden spring on the brow to burst forth through the ground, its waters carrying the child to its death. His mother, heartbroken, died from grief within days. The king decreed that the two should be laid to rest together in a nearby hamlet which afterwards became known as 'The place where Oswald by his Mother lay'. In time this was corrupted to the place we now know as Osmotherly, the start of the Lyke Wake Walk.

WAINSTONES

Perched high on the northern perimeter of the Moors, overlooking the Cleveland plain, this outcrop of rock probably provokes more emotional curses from the walking fraternity than any other throughout the British Isles. For they lie across the path of the infamous Lyke Wake Walk, at a critical point regardless of in which direction you might be attempting the feat. If the gruelling 42-mile walk across hostile and varied terrain – which incidentally has to be begun at the midnight hour and completed within twenty-four hours – is tackled in the more popular way from the inland point to the coast, then the steep and treacherous ascent through the stones occurs about 12 miles from the off. This usually means it is still dark, and the adventurous spirit which accompanied those first jaunty steps has been well and truly extinguished. The other direction obviously therefore involves descent, which to the armchair observer, must seem infinitely preferable. However, by that time, your mind is numbed by tiredness, and your limbs rubbery, from 30 miles of energy-sapping spongy moorland bog. You weave down through the razor sharp rocks, for all the world acting as though you've just finished a rather extensive ale-quaffing expedition.

I particularly remember the first time I completed the walk as a thirteen-year-old. It had rained continuously, so that by the time the ascent was made we had the unique discomfort of cold wet adhesive clothing. At the top there was a thick fog, making each step dangerous with the sheer drops barely feet away. The originators of the walk, with wry black humour, had adopted a coffin as an emblem for it because it follows the ancient funeral ways. Believe me, several times during that walk I would gladly have welcomed the relief of a life size badge!

Though it was a very frightening experience for me, during which I vowed never again to walk over any countryside, I subsequently completed it in the reverse direction, and enjoy tramping the hills more than ever now. But the Wainstones are indelibly filed under the 'horrors' heading in my memory cabinets, even though at the time of the photograph the gulley looks almost romantic under its blanket of snow. On this occasion though there was no way I was going to descend.

MIDDLESBROUGH TRANSPORTER BRIDGE

We're an ancient race in Yorkshire, tha knows. Many of our major conurbations, and come to think of it the minor ones too, are steeped in history, but this place is an exception. Look at an 1820s map of Yorkshire and you'll have to look very hard for Middlesbrough. In fact you'd be forgiven for thinking the dot which indicates its whereabouts is an ink slodge made by a nervous student cartographer. About that time the population was no more than about forty souls, living in what was described by one topographer as 'a dreary flat on an undredged river'. Then, in 1829, six Quaker entrepreneurs bought land on the south bank of the Tees. From that beginning the town and industry grew rapidly in parallel, coal, steel, shipbuilding, all utilizing the river mouth to the full. Although the shipyards, ore, and coal fields declined, the city itself successfully transferred its affections to chemicals. Parts of the outskirts have now been transformed by vast landscapes of shining silver spheroids, and cuboids, all linked by a metallic maze of pipes, making the whole structure seem more suited to the colonization of a distant planet. This assault on the eyes, and its by-product, the permanent haze of pollution which hangs like a shroud over the city, makes me think of another set of oids, with which I could liken the effect these structures have had on the environment – haemorrhoids!

In its relatively short life, Middlesbrough has been through many troughs and peaks on the industrial roller coaster. On the way satellites such as Billingham have suffered irreversible decline leaving pockets of high unemployment, and the city itself has not emerged unscathed. Amidst the visible scars, the acres of savaged wasteland, the overgrown rail sidings and dilapidated warehouses, there still lie veritable jewels of industrial heritage. This transporter bridge is one such. Until the recent renovation of a similar bridge in Newport, this was the only working one of its kind in the world. Built in 1911, and looking for all the world like an anorexic Forth Railway Bridge, this product of an overgrown Meccano set spans the river on spidery legs, and transports vehicles by a platform suspended at the end of steel hawsers. By virtue of its structure, the photographer will find its maze of interconnecting steelwork, nuts, bolts, and wires provides endless opportunities for creating simple design patterns, which often make very pleasing images. The one here is relatively simple, but obviously the wider the variation of lenses, the more infinite the possibilities.

TEESSIDE

If there's one thing I've learned it's that in the great order of things, no matter how much you try, it is impossible to find an ideal balance. Any compromise, in either personal or professional associations, inevitably means that someone somewhere will suffer.

I've always regarded Teesside as living proof of this. The loss of industry has created vast areas of dereliction to assault the eyes, and unemployment which in turn has bred boredom, depression and increased crime, and yet investment and the revival of industry almost certainly leads to high levels of pollution. For the inhabitants of such areas, it really is a case of Hobson's Choice: either to suffer long-term ill-health through continuous chemical inhalation, or through the stress that living on the breadline creates. Whilst I'm sure that the inhabitants of Teesside are justly proud of their conurbations, I could never live in such a place.

I do, however, find it interesting to visit. Decaying drab symbols of the old; bright, graphic symbols of the new; or perhaps a combination and contrast of the two. So many potential subjects can be found, no matter what medium you intend to capture it with. Take heed though, it's best to equip yourself with a particularly insensitive pair of nostrils, or visit when you are in the throes of a heavy cold, because as in this picture, all too often the waste disposal system is old, too old to cope with the pressures of the new requirements.

Perhaps though it's not as bad as first seems, because the seagulls appear to thrive on the situation, swooping and diving into the frequent effluent outflows. Though if they've flown the short distance from the North Sea it'll probably be the lesser of two evils. . . .

NORTH SEA FISHING BOAT

It's inevitable that as my upbringing occurred close to the sea, it should be the sea to which I always return for sanctuary. I've always found the cliffs, the sand, the sound of the waves to be most therapeutic. I remember when I worked in London that I regularly used to return for a dose of their tranquillizing effects. Even after three long years I never became accustomed to the speed of life, the crushing races of the Underground, and the perpetually unfriendly faces of the metropolis.

I'd spend the early mornings on the cliffs north of Scarborough watching boats set sail through the shimmering waves for various fishing grounds, and whilst the grains of sand slipped through my fingers, imagine how much more romantic it would be as a deckhand pulling those nets than working in a stuffy London studio. Of course, I never thought about those many essential trips when the prevailing weather conditions were less than idyllic. Still having to work the trawls in high running seas and all the dangers therein, whilst dodging and crashing waves, when the wind bit deep through clothing, freezing one to the bone, and fingers turned blue. Or having constantly to hack away the ice which persistently formed on the top deck between regular duties, to prevent it making sufficient weight to capsize the boat. These harsh realities of a profession which seemed romantic every time the fishing fleets unloaded their massive catches of fish were never considered. But isn't it the case that we often ignore realities if they tend to sully our dream. Unfortunately, now even the dream has gone, because thanks to fishing policies the fleets no longer exist, the weather-beaten fisherfolk faces are a scarce sight, and usually it's only a solitary boat that will brave the elements to bring the food of the deep to our table.

REDCAR

One end of Redcar has spacious promenades, amusement arcades, a golden beach, and pleasing hotels: the other has this, the expansion of Teesside's industry, encroaching onto the sand-dunes. Nevertheless, people obviously still come to this caravan camp, which just goes to show the Great British Holidaymaker's determination to have a good time regardless of the obstacles. This area seems to bear the brunt of my negative view of Yorkshire. Sadly, through the need to sustain a growing population, it has had to lay itself at the mercy of all manner of entrepreneurial talents, most of whom tend to fatten wallets with scant regard to the environment. I realize that with technological progress, there are bound to be scars to our landscape, but the pursuit of profits seems to have led to excessive rape and desecration of the extreme northern corner of my county by all and sundry. What is worse, even in this Green-aware era, it still continues, perpetrated by seemingly deaf authorities.

Among all our European partners we remain the only ones to permit a CFC poisons boat to burn off its deadly cargo whilst patrolling up and down the east coast. We are informed by Government voices that this is necessary in the interests of our prosperity, and not only do we stupidly accept this verbal sewage, but we also accept much of the real thing: London's bowels are regularly transported here to be dumped in the North Sea. We can't blame foreigners though, considering the example set by our own establishment. I refer, in particular, to the newly-privatized Yorkshire Water, presently building a new waste disposal outfall at my home town, Scarborough. It will discharge untreated sewage a short distance from the shore into tidal currents that will quickly ensure its return to the beaches. This in an area which has already seen the denial to the present generation of my own childhood pastime of picking shellfish suppers. As I see it, North Yorkshire territorial waters are in danger of becoming the ecological dustbin of Europe!

SALTBURN

There's not much to this place as a holiday resort – though I'd better clarify that statement before the burghers of the town manacle me to the pier supports, leaving me at the mercy of the incoming tide. But compared with its bigger sisters up or down the coast it's true. Here there are no amusement arcades, or hair-raising rides and the like; all you have is the paint-peeled old pier, the odd ice-cream kiosk, and flat stoneless sands. The pier is now but a shadow of its former self after years of battering by relentless violent storms, and the hand of man, which physically shortened it as a wartime precaution. However, at low tide its underbelly and the pools of water around its legs offer interesting photographic potential. The real reason I included it though, is that in spite of the number of tourist resorts we boast, it remains the only pier to grace the Yorkshire coastline. Above, and staring contemptuously down is a line of Victorian buildings, the jewel of which is the Zetland Hotel. It is a seaside town of the old-fashioned variety, when the simple pleasures of sand and sea, listening to band concerts, walking in the gardens, or lazing in the sea-front shelters were sufficient to constitute a complete holiday. Perhaps there may have been a candy-striped Punch and Judy booth, to amuse the children.

I met a P. and J. operator recently and apparently the entertainment is making a come-back. He's part of a kind of society, and in his case the stint is a working holiday, escaping from a boring southern city job. That's the way to do it! Sadly though, he finds, though popular with the kids, he is encountering strong opposition to the revival from some quarters. Probably the same people who think Noddy is a racist.

That's what Saltburn is, a trip back into a much more relaxed way of life, probably still nearer to the way Henry Pease saw it in 1856 than 1991. It was his Saltburn Improvement Company which brought the railway here and transformed a fishing village into a resort. He even provided a personal station for the Zetland when it was finished so that privileged hotel residents could step direct from carriage to lobby. The place also played a part in British amateur sporting tradition, for these flat sands were at one stage considered by Malcolm Campbell as the venue for one of his world land speed record-breaking runs. Unfortunately, probably because of the unpredictability of the weather, he decided in favour of Daytona.

BOULBY CLIFFS

These cliffs, which rise to a height of almost 700 feet, are reputed to be the highest in England. There are a few who dispute their right to that title, but as they are obviously not Yorkshire folk, they don't count. It is said that they were named after Beowulf the Norse warrior, who, as befits his reputation, demanded that he should be buried on the highest cliffs, and so was brought here. However, though excavations have been made at various times, no remains have ever been found to verify that this is his resting place.

Not only is this the best place to view them in all their splendour, but it also happens to be easily accessible by car. But take care because the winding little cliff-top road which leaves the main Staithes to Saltburn thoroughfare for the hamlet of Cowbar in parts passes just a few feet from the edge. To look at the cliffs from here your back will be to Staithes and the coastline below, so obviously you'll be facing north. Well, logically, that's what the map states. Yet, just look at the right hand side of the scene – that's the sun beginning its descent. But the sun sets in the west! Actually, it's a strange quirk caused by the indented meanderings of the coastline hereabouts, so that you can never be quite sure exactly which way you are facing. At certain times of the year it's possible to watch the sun rise, and set, over the North Sea.

The chimneyed establishment on the left is Boulby Mine, which has the deepest shaft in Europe at 4000 feet. It mines potash for use in the fertilizing industry but is now near to being worked out. Not too long ago, there was uproar after a 'leak' that because of its depth and the rock strata type, the shafts had been bored out under the sea, and it was therefore being considered as a suitable ready-made dump for nuclear waste. This, of course, has been vehemently denied by various government departments.

KETTLENESS

It's time to don those climbing boots, fill a rucksack with flask, Kendal mint cake, and rainproofs and mentally prepare for a long haul. Actually I've cheated, by lying on my stomach, complete with wide angle lens, so it's not as high as it seems. It's probably only about 50 feet or so to the top, but the shale makes a jolly good surface to run up and slide down!

The various mounds and a few foundation stones are all that survive of a once thriving alum-mining community on the kettleness promontory. Alum was used as a fixing agent in the cloth-dyeing process. This was the second hamlet here, built in 1831, the original cluster of workers' cottages having disappeared during a great storm in 1829, when heavy rain undermined the clay cliff and it slid into the sea. At that time the industry was still important enough for it to be rebuilt, but eventually a cheaper substitute was found to replace the alum. This was probably inevitable, since about 100 tons of the raw material yielded only a few tons of the purified product.

The whole area resembles what I imagine a moonscape looks like. I've used its grey surface once or twice for fashion backgrounds, and I've often wondered how eerie it might look under the silver light of the moon. Trouble is I daren't visit at night because there's a local tale that the spectre of a massive headless hound stalks the mounds, and I'm just enough of a coward not even to attempt to prove the legend isn't true – just in case it could be!

STAITHES

There have always been three styles of fishing from the Yorkshire shores. The big trawling fleets, now no more, worked out of Hull. These would be gone for perhaps two or three weeks at a time, travelling far up around Iceland and other Arctic climes. The smaller boats of Scarborough and Whitby, also now depleted through economics, would only be gone for three or four days, and venture no further than the North Sea. But these boats the Cobles, working from any navigable inlet, would be away for only perhaps a day or a night. Never far from shore, not only would they fish for finned animals, but also lay lobster pots. Like the rest of the fishing industry, even the owners of these boats have suffered to some extent, but a lucrative niche in the tourist industry has to a certain extent offset this. It seems quite a popular holiday pastime now, to get a group together, hire a boat, and spend the days bobbing up and down.

Staithes was where young James Cook, later the famous Captain, learned his first skills, and the cottage where he was apprenticed still exists, as does the custom of the fishermen's wives of wearing Staithes bonnets while they sit and knit their unique ganseys (jumpers). I love to wander round the village, because much of it appears unchanged from the time the great Frank Meadow Sutcliffe made it the subject of his cumbersome equipment. It's a challenge to try to recreate some of the mood of his greatest work, though I regard it as an almost impossible task. For I do not profess to have his vision, and neither do I have his primitive emulsions. Today's technologically superb films do not seem to have the ambience of those early self-coated glass plates.

WHITBY HARBOUR

For the most part you won't be distracted by seaside entertainments here. True there are a couple of 'token' arcades but for the most part Whitby is an 'amusement-free zone'. It allows you to wander leisurely, and slake your intellectual thirst. Perhaps in the Abbey, or nearby St Mary's, the interior of which was built in the likeness of a ship by craftsmen who fashioned the real thing below in the harbour, and the exterior of which is filled with weather-worn gravestones telling sea tales of sadness and heroism. Learn of Caedmon, father of English poetry, or Captain Cook who left here to chart unknown lands.

You could if you wanted walk on the sands and, like Lewis Carroll, who is reputed to have made regular day trips here when he lived at Croft on Teesside, you too might see the Walrus and the Carpenter, though I think you'd be more likely to find some Whitby jet. Small pieces are still found here, brought in on the tide. If you are unlucky, you could buy some from one of the few local carvers in the old town who still fashion jet, the stone first having been made fashionable by the mourning Queen Victoria. At least here you could be sure it was genuine and not some cheap imitation like that a market trader in London tried to sell me once. Funny how 'It's the real thing Guv' suddenly lost interest in a sale when he discovered where I came from. He needn't have worried; I doubt if I could tell the difference, though I'm led to believe that good jet is warm to touch, and turns brown under a flame.

Whitby to me, though, is the tradition of seafaring through the centuries, and I love to watch a high sea here, how the harbour entrance can suddenly transform raging waves into a safe haven of docile ripples. Two extremities of one of nature's most potent forces, separated only by a thin concrete barrier. It may have been like this to the eye of Bram Stoker, when he visualized the storm which awakened Dracula, the Prince of Darkness: the boat passing from maelstrom to calm between those twin lighthouses, crewless save for a headless seaman lashed to the wheel; the black dog leaping to shore, racing up 199 steps to rest in the refuge of a grave just by our viewpoint, until disturbed by dear Lucy Harker.

ROBIN HOOD'S BAY

Do you believe in legends wholeheartedly? Or do you, like me, wonder if some are created to enhance the quaint appeal of a place to the tourist industry? Several legends connect Baytown, as it is affectionately referred to by locals, to the outlaw. One in particular bears a striking resemblance to the way in which he was supposed to have chosen his final resting place. Wanting somewhere to live he went to the highest cliff and loosed off an arrow, declaring that where it landed he would build a home, and hence eventually a community grew around it. Perhaps the Earl of Locksley was indeed a man given to a life run on whims and fate, and there is after all some truth in how the village was founded.

One thing is certain, the community has managed successfully to reach that delicate balance, which is all too rare, of appealing to tourism, whilst still retaining its natural charm. Indeed, it is probably now much as it was in the early parts of this century, when the resident Leo Walmsley used it as the model for Bramblewick in *Sea Fever,* and other novels, subsequently filmed as *Turn of the Tide*. Perhaps the only real addition is the sea wall, but this was necessary, because in its precarious position on the cliff the town had lost several streets and numerous cottages over a period of time through erosion.

The place has always had an attraction for the culturally artistic, and in its time has spawned many insular communities which followed the prevailing trends. It's as such that I have my happiest memories of the place, for in the late sixties, I, like most others of my age, aspired to become a rock star. The group was formed and as the other members came from the Bay, this is where we were based and rehearsed. I remember many a pub crawl round all of its three hostelries, under the pretence of seeking inspiration. Now whenever I take time out to wander through its maze of back alleys, around every corner there is a reminder of those flower-power days, and the echoes of the 'sounds' we made come back to haunt me. One thing about the place even now is that it provides many characters all too willing to entertain for a drink or two, from the old fisherman, to the beachcomber who still seeks out jet to carve after every high tide, quite successfully too I may add.

SCARBOROUGH HARBOUR

The occasional cry of a circling gull as it awaits the return of its floating fast food takeaway; the lapping of the lazy tide against the harbour wall; the creaking of the tired timbers of old boats as they ride the gentle swell. Soothing sounds which are carried by the cool breeze of salt air, mildly fragranced with the bouquet of seaweed and fish, as the warm glow of the setting sun bathes the whole scene. Romantic, relaxing, unwinding, that's why I love my returns to Scarborough.

Admittedly, it's very difficult to experience this in the summer months when it's more likely to be the tensely irritating shrill of hypnotic cacophony of mind-warping laser-phaser machines and the lingering odours of sweat-diluted sun tan lotion or stale fish 'n' chips which accompany your evening stroll through forests of discarded food wrappings. But, they say, '*C'est la vie*', and the price to pay for an affluent town. Not so, because the charm of the place, evident in the winter months, need not have been so savaged and devoured if successive council fathers had not worn the hats of representative of the people, and of greedy entrepreneur at the same time. But that's the way it's always been in our borough.

In much the same way these 'guardians' of our treasures have successfully accomplished with bureaucratic ease what both the Kaiser and Hitler failed to do. They have allowed most structures of beauty and architectural heritage to be demolished and replaced by sterile obscenities fresh from the dreams of incapable architects. You think I jest, that I exaggerate the wanton official vandalism. I do not, for what happened to the Floral Hall – replaced by a 'box' of bowls; Christ Church: a frozen food centre; the Balmoral Hotel: a multi-storey car-park and supermarket; the Pavilion Hotel, once the home of Tom Laughton, and his Hollywood actor brother Charles: a bland box of windows to house among others the Department of Unemployment. The latest atrocity, but I'm afraid unlikely to be the last, was against an old department store and a Georgian terrace, both bulldozed to make way for a gargantuan shopping arcade of brick and glass. You've heard of the proverbial white elephant, well this I think is destined to provide a whole herd.

CAYTON BAY

Though the vast sweeping bay south of Scarborough now boasts several caravan sites along its rim, these are fortunately unobtrusive enough to be invisible should you stand on its sandy shoreline. We hear so much today about the Greenhouse Effect and the higher flood tides this will inevitably produce, but here is an outstanding example of how the tidal movements must have varied over the centuries regardless of these twentieth-century phenomena. Particularly after spring-tides, evidence like this appears, testifying to previous forestation. These decaying old stumps, the remains of trees suffocated by the deposit of sand and silt by the waves, are now being revealed again by the very same sea. I've no doubt that perhaps in a million years they will provide the black jet treasures that future beachcombers will seek.

A hundred years ago, the richer visitor might have had elegant leisurely strolls through the wooded area of this and the adjacent bay, perhaps occasionally glancing at their feet in the hope of finding a small red cornelian stone. Personally about twenty-five years ago I could never have that lethargic pleasure, because the area formed a particularly strenuous part of my school's standard cross-country run. The only perk was that coming half-way through the course, the sparse woodland which had escaped the sea's ravages provided meagre camouflage for a brief breather and a crafty fag.

FILEY BRIGG

The outcrop of Filey Brigg, which penetrates half a mile into the North Sea, is a very popular location for naturalists and geologists. Unfortunately it's also a very treacherous area for those in, and out of, boats. There's a long history of wrecks, drawn onto its jagged rocks by powerful currents, and for unwary foot visitors it can also be deceiving – for you can stand well along its length safely dodging the waves, whilst nearer to shore the Brigg will already have been breached, cutting off your escape route. Warnings of the danger are often ignored in favour of the thrill of scrambling and playing cat and mouse with the malevolent whitecaps. I know, because my friends and I regularly entertained ourselves here in our youth.

Folklore suggests that the peninsula was formed by the Devil, who intended to provide himself with an above water version of the Channel Tunnel, but he failed to complete it. Obviously he couldn't find anyone willing to pour money into such a foolish venture! But people hereabouts know the real story. It began one night when a drunken tailor by the name of Billy Biter was returning home. He'd had one too many, to numb his senses to the inevitable nagging of his wife, and fell into the local dragon's lair. As you can imagine, Old Smokey was none too pleased at being awakened from his dreams of frying damsels. In fear of being devoured, Billy offered some of his wife's treacle parkin as appeasement. As an hors-d'oeuvre to the main meal cowering before him, the dragon accepted gleefully. What the creature didn't know was that Billy's wife's parkin had a fearful reputation; indeed Filey fishermen used it for caulking their boats. Within seconds his jaws were inextricably fixed together, and, fiery breath bringing tears to his eyes, he rushed towards the sea hoping it might nullify the substance's adhesive quality. Unfortunately, in the dark he tripped over a daisy, and tumbled head over tail down the cliff to drown in the rising tide. No one was able to move his scaly body, which eventually petrified to form the Brigg.

FLAMBOROUGH HEAD

Look at these white cliffs. Aren't they at least the equal to those at Dover? Careful though, the edge here is very crumbly! The danger signs shouldn't really be ignored, but this spot does give the best panorama of the cliffs. R.D. Blackmore was familiar with this area and used it as the setting for his novel *Mary Anerley: A Yorkshire Tale* in 1880. Though not as well known as *Lorna Doone*, it is worth reading for his descriptions not only of the landscape, but also of the people and the community of the time. Flamborough won't look like this for long, though, with the sunlight sparkling on the chalk, because just beyond the stack is that East Coast phenomenon, a sea fret. When the tide rushes in, the cold air above meets the warm land air and forms a thick white mist. It swirls around the coves, enveloping them and blotting out the sun here, just as it often does right along the coast. Not that it stops holiday-makers enjoying themselves: many's the time I've seen beaches full of them stretched out, determined to sunbathe despite being unable to see as far as the next group of deckchairs!

It's a shame really, because it means the rock formations and sea water pools below are hidden. There is an abundance of interesting graphically colourful patterns here, which are superb for close-up photography. I've spent many hours wandering around here with a macro lens. The grey curtain also prevents us from seeing beyond the headland, where the American privateer John Paul Jones's ship was engaged and sunk by the Royal Navy. Though not before, in true Hollywood swashbuckling tradition, he and his crew boarded and captured one of the British ships.

RUDSTON

This tiny Wolds hamlet is perhaps best known as the novelist Winifred Holtby's resting place, and the background against which her best-known novel, *South Riding*, was played. Indeed the television adaptation which did so much to rekindle the popularity of her work, was filmed predominantly on location here. However, for me, its most striking feature is the monolith, which throws up many puzzling and confusing questions.

Firstly, if it is genuinely primitive, how did a tribe with no knowledge of even the simple mechanics of a block and tackle, manage to erect it? Though no one seems to have tried to prove the fact conclusively, perhaps it is a 'stone iceberg' with at least as much again of its 25 foot height buried under the ground. Perhaps a great hole could have been dug, equal to half its length, into which it was then toppled, so that its natural momentum would draw it upright. Pity the poor devils who then had to fill in the hole to prevent it falling back over again.

Secondly, if it was erected as a place of worship, then to what? The underground spring called the Gypsy Race which flows from here to the sea at Bridlington harbour perhaps? If their water authority was like ours, seeming to be unprepared for long hot spells, then perhaps the provision of an unfailing spring freeing them from the threat of a drought deserved such a mark of respect?

Thirdly, and to my mind most intriguing, if it was a site of ancient pagan worship, why has a religious authority built a place of Christian worship around it? To prove perhaps that it is stronger than any heathen religion? To remind fickle congregations of the possible outcome of any waivering of the strength of their faith?

I love anything which by its presence, provokes intriguing questions. It's probably why I have been drawn to the Rudston monolith on more than one occasion.

BEVERLEY MINSTER

When I look around my county, I might be excused for wondering whether we were responsible for the sustenance of Christianity in the British Isles. For although there are many older sites connected with religion, we do seem to have the greatest concentration of minsters, abbeys, cathedrals and priories. In ruined state we are well represented with many internationally-famous remains, and we don't do too badly in existing gothic beauties either. However there are many in our broad acres which don't get the praise they deserve. For example Ripon Cathedral, Selby Abbey, and the minsters of Stonegrave and St Gregory – the former reputed to be the smallest of its kind in the land, and the latter retaining excellent features of Norman architecture, both almost hidden away in the depths of Ryedale.

But my representative of practising Houses of God must fall to Beverley Minster. On the outside much of the work dates from medieval times, particularly the east end of about 1220 and the west tower of the fifteenth century. However it is the interior at which I marvel. There is an abundance of stone and wood carvings adorning the tombs: rural scenes on the misericords crafted from Sherwood Forest oak, the canopy of the Percy tomb with its fourteenth-century effigies of angels, fruits and beasts, and lead statues of St John of Beverley. These are just a few of the treasures on which one's eyes can feast. My personal interest in such places is not in these intricate details, however, but in the general designs which can be found by altering viewpoints amongst the pillars, and combining them with the roof. What really excites me though is that even this chosen perspective will then give continuous variations because of the subtle contrast changes provided by the natural stained-glass window illumination.

SPURN POINT

A long thin spit of land, Spurn Point snakes out into the North Sea, then, as if having second thoughts about its journey into the inhospitable deep, curves round in an arc but never quite reaches the mainland again. In places it is only 40 to 50 feet wide at high tide, and barely resists the erosive power of the sea. Indeed, on more than one occasion in the last few years, storms have breached it completely, breaking up the concrete spine. The road which leads along it to the isolated lifeboat community at its end has perhaps prevented Spurn from disappearing completely, but the precariousness of it has finally prompted a decision to relocate the lifeboat and coastguard stations. When they are finally moved and the families no longer need to be protected as they go to mainland shops and schools, the community will probably eventually join its predecessors beneath the waves.

One of the ancient communities which the sea claimed, and which now lies somewhere under the mud banks off the point, was Ravenspurn. Known to Shakespeare, this was the place where in 1399, Henry of Lancaster landed to claim the throne, and where seventy years later Edward IV set foot on English soil from Dutch exile to end the Wars of the Roses. It's debatable even to this day whether he succeeded, because Lancastrians still try hard to dispute their undoubted inferiority to us!

The disappearance of the point would be lamented by many, particularly 'twitchers' for whom the RSPB nature reserve has become a very important observation post of many rare species. Even for those like me, who have no fanatical interest in birds, it will still be a sad loss. There's a peculiar solitude, even with the large volume of ships which ply the Humber estuary, or the other beach strollers who share the coarse sand with you. It always reminds me of Masefield's famous poem, 'Sea Fever'. His words echo on the wind as it whistles round the rotting groynes, reminding me of the monotonous loneliness, the vicious unpredictability, and the callous strength of the sea's unrelenting motion.

STONE CREEK, HUMBER ESTUARY

'The Humber rough and stout' observed Edmund Spenser way back in 1586. Since that time few have had particularly good words to say about the river, which has never been regarded with the romance afforded to others of its ilk like the Thames or the Avon. I must admit that its murky tidal waters probably wouldn't have the same inspirational qualities as the latter, and one wonders if Shakespeare, had he been born to this region, would have composed such literary classics had he been seated on the banks of the Humber!

It's not half as dirty as it used to be though, since a conscious effort has been made on the part of industrialists; in fact, fish now have a reasonable chance of survival within its waters. The river does not deserve to be as much maligned as it has been, for it sports one of the largest suspension bridges in the world, the beautiful city of Hull, and the vast expanse of Spurn. Also, as a sea river of importance, it has long played its part in bringing prosperity to the whole country, and has secured enough memorable places in British maritime history to rival any other. Some of the greatest whaling expeditions began along this stretch, as did the fatal voyage of the *Bounty*, with one Captain Bligh at the helm.

I must admit that the vast stretches of muddy banks, broken by rows of duck-like cranes can look obnoxious, but there are along its shores quiet little havens. Some like Paull, its lighthouse built in 1830 and reputed to be one of the oldest in the British Isles, have special points of interest while others serving Sunday sailors, provide pleasant walks. In addition to being visually interesting because of the contrast between modern and ancient harbour techniques, this creek also has the dubious distinction of being last resting place for a pair of my old wellies. In order to reach the best perspective vantage point on a particular boat, I ventured too far into the quagmire. Though with great difficulty I managed to alleviate that sinking feeling, the aforementioned objects of attire became inextricably stuck forever. I wonder what some twenty-second century archaeologist might make of that find!

CITY CENTRE, HULL

Its origin as Kingstown upon the river Hull was as long ago as 1293, when it was created a port by Edward I, yet Hull always seems to be regarded as a modern city. Part of the reason probably lies in the fact that much of it had to be totally rebuilt after the Second World War. My grandfather was stationed on barrage balloons in the estuary during the war and related horrific tales of the bombardments which turned the city into a sea of fire, and reduced its buildings to rubble. In fact, though London and Coventry were, and still are, regarded as symbolic of ordinary people's resistance to the Nazi war machine, neither received the concentrated attention the Luftwaffe afforded this city.

I admit that I too was inclined to regard it as modern until 1983, when I was invited by the local newspaper to produce a series of photographs for a calendar. An offer which worried me immensely, especially as one of the conditions was that all the work had to be derived from a 2 square mile area. I needn't have worried for, even in the present Hull, there is a great deal of old architecture and history. Though it's not as old as York, I think it can rival it admirably.

Hull is one of those places that was taken for granted, and not fully appreciated until it went. Hence, when it was carved away in 1974, at the whim of a politician, and its inhabitants forced to relinquish their right to be called Yorkshirepersons, the uproar was tremendous. Even now sixteen years on, the whole affair leaves a bitter taste in Yorkshire mouths, and Humberside exists only in the imagination of Westminster.

I pondered long and hard as to how I could best illustrate the maritime pride of north, west, and east Yorkshire. At first I thought of King Billy's dazzling golden statue. He who, so folklore relates, goes walkabout every night, but will only fail to return before sun up should some catastrophe be about to overtake the city. Eventually I moved a short way up the road to Holy Trinity Church, much of which still retains the original fourteenth-century architecture. To see it reflected in this glass expanse of more current design, epitomizes the spirit of, and pride in, the city – a place where antiquity and current are blended by the city fathers into acceptable harmony.

FERRYBRIDGE

There's a fair few of these great monsters stretched across the bottom of Yorkshire, cooling towers constantly billowing out great clouds of steam, whilst the reclaimed water runs down into the collecting tanks to be reused. They are part of a continual cycle as they strive to meet the power needs of our televisions, washing machines and electric kettles. In this modern age of controversial nuclear reactors, I suppose stations can be built almost anywhere, but before now it seemed natural that these sustaining hearts of the nation should be built on or near the coal seams.

On a really clear day, the station can be seen from high on the North Yorkshire Moors, a good 25 miles away, but strangely when travelling from the south it makes a sudden appearance. When I lived in London, I to'd and fro'd past it often, and have seen it in a very wide variety of weather conditions and moods. And even if it's lit by brilliant sunshine, there's still a sinister foreboding air about it: something menacing. This great hideous monstrosity of technology, which by its very existence desecrates the skyline, should provoke a contemptuous attitude towards it. Yet, perversely, it actually endears itself because I have always regarded it as an emotional trigger. Homeward bound the traveller, I finally know when I see those great inverted concrete vases that once again my body has reached where my heart always lies. Even though I've actually already been in God's county for some miles. . . .

FITZWILLIAM — GEOFF BOYCOTT'S BIRTHPLACE

This looks like any ordinary back-to-back terraced street, typical of many throughout the country, particularly if, like this one, they once nurtured a closed mining community. These may have been modernized somewhat, but they are still of no architectural importance. So what is the significance of this unremarkable thoroughfare in the great Yorkshire history?

The dwellings may be modest by certain criteria, the lamp-post undramatic, and the smattering of discarded refuse less sophisticated than that of a Mayfair gutter, but this street is a shrine. It's a peculiar trait of the character of Yorkshire people, that the mention of the word 'cricket' — whether as individuals, they love the game, or find a team wielding bits of wood trying to prevent another team from hitting a lump of leather with other bits of wood pointless and boring — will set pulses racing with the fluid of patriotic fervour, and a passionate pride that invariably escalates into argument, controversy, and speculation, to such extremes that even brother might be set against brother, in a way that no one outside the Broad Acres could begin to understand. Which county cricket supporter, living away would return to have his baby born within his county so that it would be eligible to play for it if it were a boy? Only a Yorkshire supporter. . . .

This is the birthplace of Geoffrey Boycott, arguably the greatest batsman ever to stand astride the crease for county and country, and whose dedication to and love for his county game is beyond question, but yet is alternately branded champion, hero, scapegoat, and transgressor, by a fickle warring cricket committee.

I used the camera trickery of slow shutter speed to blurr the passer-by for a reason. Sadly it signifies the Ghost of Yorkshire Cricket — when the argument was how easily we would win, and not, have we even a chance of winning. I hope the hierarchy of our club realizes that if they'd had just a fraction of the pride in Yorkshire that Boycott and others they have similarly vilified and cast out had, then we might still today have been a force to strike fear into opponents' hearts.

PIT HEAD, BARNSLEY

The mention of Yorkshire conjures up for some images of cramped pit villages over-shadowed by satanic black pit heads, from which emerge shift after shift of soot 'n' sweat-streaked miners after toiling in atrocious conditions at the coal face; of those same workers singing while scrubbing away the grime in old tin baths by the fire; of the dreaded sirens heralding underground accidents which often obliterated whole families. Or perhaps the pre-war film scenario has been replaced by images of ignorant, pig headed, violent troublemakers intent on continually causing unrest with their strikes and picket lines. I prefer to believe that it is merely stubbornness fighting for what is to them the just cause of better conditions and secure employment.

In such confrontations, there are heroes who become villains, and inevitably by virtue of our natural Yorkshire aggression, they are from this county. I neither condemn nor condone the actions of 'King' Arthur Scargill, having only press reports to make judgement. Right or wrong, I hope that whatever he has done, as a truly dedicated Yorkshireman, was with the best intention of protecting the welfare of his miners. Whatever we think of him or his methods, the frightening aspect is that at least one of his predictions could be becoming reality: the eventual destruction of British mining.

I suggest this because of what I have seen while producing this book. I searched for this typical scene which is so often associated with Yorkshire, intending it to be a tribute to the hardy miners, who have given their lives through the years, keeping the home fires burning in war and peace. Four years ago, when working on the illustrations for *Hillaby's Yorkshire*, I found several locations for shots. This time I searched in vain, every shaft wheel now dismantled and the pit closed. Enquiries in what was once the heart of the coal belt brought bewilderment as to where I might find one now. The location I eventually found in Barnsley was even as I captured it in the process of demolition. Love him or hate him, King Arthur might just have foreseen the end of an industry, sunk by the flood of foreign coal. I just hope that the illustration which was intended to celebrate the Yorkshire mining tradition, will not prove to be an epitaph.

HEPTONSTALL

I really like this place because it's been preserved in an untampered state; there have been no 'renovations' or 'modernizations' to detract from the atmosphere of old Yorkshire. The textile village is reputed to be one of the finest remaining examples of its kind in the West Riding and I, for one, agree with that. On a high crag, surrounded by moorland, it preceded the coming of railway, canal and mechanized textile production by a long chalk. A place which sets the mind racing, helped in no small way by the custom of dating buildings on the lintels. Who inhabited the White Hall in 1578? What must it have been like to have attended the Grammar school in 1642? In this particular case an exercise of the imagination which is admirably helped along by the preservation of desks, books, etc.

The religious establishments of Heptonstall are reason enough for a visit here. The octagonal chapel, built to John Wesley's own specification in 1764, is the oldest of its kind still in use. Apparently it was so advanced in design that no one locally could produce the roof, so it had to be assembled in Rotherham and transported here by carts. Being brought up a Methodist, it is obviously of particular interest to me, as is the amazing fact that the following was so strong at one time that the Sunday school here had over a thousand pupils. Back home, even on a good Sunday we couldn't have provided the disciples for a passion play!

Just across the way is the present church, built amidst the ruins of its fifteenth-century predecessor. The graveyard is a treasure for headstone-hunters. Some roguish stories emerge from these resting places, like that of Hartley, 'King of the Coiners', who was executed for doubling the value of gold coins. Today he'd be knighted for enterprise! Sad stories too, for here is buried American poetess Sylvia Plath, who committed suicide after a short turbulent life. She came to know the area as the wife of Ted Hughes, himself a native.

ORPHANS' GRAVE

The remnants of the booming textile industry look very picturesque, situated as they are amid woodland or moorland, by the many tiny gurgling streams which were so essential to the existence of the furnaces and the clanking spinning looms. As such, they present a very false impression to the tourists of today: perhaps we might not be so anxious to point our cameras at these relics, if the images captured showed a true picture of how it was when the mills were at full capacity. Imagine if every frame returned from the one-hour development service, portrayed some different aspect of these profit-making workshops, each one guaranteed to turn the stomach in disbelieving revulsion; if each vividly depicted the atrocious conditions in which women and children had to toil day-in day-out to provide their masters with the wherewithal to sustain luxurious lifestyles.

Fortunately, the united muscle of an increasingly educated workforce, with some help from the odd humane wool baron, evolved a situation, where, in this country at least, it is now impossible for my lens adequately to portray how it was. However, on the hillsides there are still poignant little reminders of that age. This is just one I discovered almost hidden in the nettles of a churchless graveyard at the end of the beautiful valley of Luddenden. The sad simple headstone marks the release from a living Hell of seven orphans, aged from only twelve years to seventeen years, who in their short tragic lives probably never really saw or experienced any of the wonders of nature which existed outside their prison, and which we now so often take for granted.

DWELLING, CALDERDALE

For obvious reasons, most of the towns that sprung up in the nineteenth century were built near to factories, and so the narrow valleys which cut the moorland were crammed as full as possible with houses. As demand increased, so the building encroached on the slopes, spreading upwards in a mass of brick and stone. The style of these cramped dwellings created a maze of tiny cobbled streets, and narrow passageways known as ginnels or snickets.

Nowadays, this industrial map of interconnecting passages provides great interest to the indulgent tourist, with the result that many of these formerly ugly conurbations have found a new source of income. Much of this has been helped in no small way by the advent of television, which having discovered the charm of such places, utilizes the locations in a glut of series, dramas, and comedies, the most famous being *Last of the Summer Wine* which seems to have done for Holmfirth what the Prince Regent did for Brighton in the popularity stakes. It's difficult to wander through the backstreets of the town now without encountering a Compo Wellie Step follower or a horde of Nora Batty Wrinkled-Stocking hunters, intent on satiating their lust with a sighting of crushed nylon!

However, there are other areas if one wants to tread the cobbles alone, and peek nosily around the yards and alleys in search of secret pigeon lofts or antique washing line props. I love to indulge in such expeditions from time to time, because not only do they provide fascinating insights into the architecture of the time, and interesting cameo scenes for my camera – but to find my way back to the start often presents a puzzle of mind-bending proportions.

SALTAIRE

The orphans' grave (page 61) testifies to the cruel inhumanity of wool barons in their quest for financial reward. But, as with every story, there are two sides, and this place is a lasting tribute to one of those rare entrepreneurs who was exceptionally philanthropic.

Sir Titus Salt was a truly enlightened man of the mid-nineteenth century, and whilst he was not averse to pocketing the proceeds, he also believed in rewarding the efforts of his workforce. When Victorian fashion dictated the need for a special cloth, he built a custom-designed factory to produce it, then the largest and most advanced in Europe. He also modernized it with new concepts, which took away much of the discomfort to the operators previously associated with such establishments: special chimneys which extracted poisonous fumes, to reduce pollution; underfloor machinery eliminating much of the damaging noise; and large plate glass windows for a bright and airy environment. If he'd stopped there, he would still have been remembered as a great innovator, but this extraordinary man believed in rewarding his employees' families too. To this end, he built a small town of houses which rejected the normal cramped conditions in favour of space. Piped water, gas, and sanitary disposal systems were connected to each abode. Corner shops with a plentiful choice of provisions, a hospital to administer to health needs, a library and schools for the education of the children completed the self-contained community.

Yet, there *was* one exclusion from the amenities: the public house. Abhorring alcohol, and its harmful effects, Salt decreed that no such establishment should be allowed to trade within the confines of his town. Some might consider the man an eccentric – after all, one of his acts was to purchase the original Trafalgar Square lions deemed too small to defend Nelson's Column, and erect them in Saltaire – but there is no doubt that to the inhabitants of the town he was a magnificent benefactor, who abolished hardship and disease. His body, resting in the mausoleum, must be tortured with mixed emotion as it watches over his pride. For though the town still stands as a tribute to his genius and social conscience, much of his mill, the instigator of it all, lies empty and derelict.

COW AND CALF ROCKS, ILKLEY MOOR

'Where has tha' bin sin ah saw thee. . . . On Ilkla Moor bah'tat.'

Even if your vocal renderings more closely resemble the regretful cries of a seen-to Tom cat than Pavarotti, this is still the place to forever endear yourself to Yorkshire's ones. Climb to these rocks perched high on the slopes, clear your lungs of the clogged air you've purloined from the industrial valleys below, and bellow out the words of our hallowed anthem. The strange looks you attract will be of admiration, not pity. Other visitors to the rocks may give you a wide berth because they are in awe of your capabilities, but you will, I assure you be awarded for this feat. Some officials in white coats will approach and present you with a special Yorkshire 'backward jacket' to straighten your posture before entering our specially padded recording studios.

'Tha's bin a corting Mary Jane, On Ilkla Moor bah'tat.'

The Moor and the stones have long been a focal point for private romantic liaisons. In fact, I bet more babies in the Leeds/Bradford area were found under Cow and Calf than under gooseberry bushes! They have also during daylight hours been the destination over many years of countless family, factory and church outings. The rocks – and I don't know why they have that name because I've looked at every angle and the only resemblance I can see is that there's a big one and a small one – carry indelible memories of these on their surface, in a multitude of carved names and dates. As I look at them, I often try to imagine the scene at the time they were written, what the graffitists were like, their lifestyles, dress, interests, and wonder how many of them may still be alive.

LEEDS MILL

From early times, the area which is now Yorkshire had a greater abundance of fleece-providing animals than other parts of the British Isles. As man progressed to the skill of weaving it spread to many of the major European centres, and being of a shrewd disposition and never slow to recognize a profitable opportunity, we soon sported men who acquired the highly-skilled techniques. And around them congregated craftsmen capable of processing the finished item from sheep's back to human's back.

However the processes were tedious and expensive until along came a number of entrepreneurial souls, including one Cartwright, who developed mechanical aids to weaving cloth. It was with the inception of these that West Yorkshire came into its own, for the machines needed power to propel them. What better than to situate them by streams, and ample seams of coal. Vast mills were built, their ever-active chimneys turning whole valleys into grimy basins of throbbing workshops. The Industrial Revolution did bring prosperity, but only to a relative few, who tended to be unaccustomed to the burden of wealth. The eccentricities of these sometimes inarticulate uncultured people can be seen in the profusion of grand ornate structures which adorn many of the towns. Usually commissioned on a whim, or to outmatch the similar 'folly' of a competitor, the diverse and, often uncomplementary styles imitated previous architectural ages.

Sadly, these financial extravagances, and costly improvements in employment conditions, left the industry unprepared for the commercial emergence of Far Eastern competition, and the ability of such as Korea to produce cloth at much lower prices sent it into serious decline. Rambling round the many decaying warehouses, or standing on dilapidated stairways such as this, there is now only evocative silence where once there was the deafening scream of weaving machinery and the idle chatter of pressers, cutters, warpers and sizers.

LEEDS–LIVERPOOL CANAL

Before the monsters of steam rattled across our fair country, and the petrol combustion engine demanded that tarmac bridleways snake into even the most inaccessible areas, transportation of people and goods depended largely on the poor horse, and a system of rutted thoroughfares. This was of course very slow, and soon a more efficient method of transfer, particularly for goods, was required. Water was a commodity freely available, and so existing rivers and ports were interconnected by building a series of man-made canals. One of the most impressive of these is the Leeds–Liverpool Canal, whose 127 miles cross the Pennine backbone of Britain. In the eighteenth and nineteenth centuries it was a link between the wool industry and the port of Liverpool. A further canal linked Leeds with Hull and so a water traverse of the whole county became available, in its heyday a vital commercial line of communication.

Today, the canal is still used commercially, particularly by coal barges to the east of Leeds, and it seems that there may be a resurgence in this relatively cheap if slightly slow form of transport. However to the west, the major use tends to be for barge holidays. The attractions on the banks of the waterway are easily accessible, and also make very pleasant day excursions. I particularly enjoy visiting it at Bingley, watching the slow progress of the barges as they negotiate the Five Rise Locks. Canals entice me because I regard them, their traffic, and much of their adjacent paraphernalia as extremely photogenic, particularly the mechanics of locks. Actually if no one has yet thought of it, this canal, with its contrasting scenery of vale, moorland, and city, would make an excellent long distance footpath.

VIRGIN BRIDGE, TADCASTER

You've probably already heard of 'Taddy', with reference to it being the brewing capital of North Yorkshire. The two Smiths, Sam and John, have long been locked in liquid war as to which is the best Yorkshire ale. John Tetley – another local brewer – might dispute the fact that either of them should lay claim to the title! I for one am not prepared to enter the debate, pass judgement, or award the crown; not being enough of an authority on mild and bitter, and preferring Theakston's Old Peculiar anyway. However, it is the brewing capital, and it has supported such industry since medieval times when it was first discovered that the hard water which flowed from magnesian limestone was particularly well suited to the production of quality alcoholic beverage.

The presence of three breweries in the vicinity gives the town a unique flavour, the atmosphere being filled with the burnt yet not distasteful aroma of hops. Before the bypass was built, I remember being frequently stuck in snail's-pace summer traffic queues at what was a notorious traffic bottleneck, in which cars' occupants soon became very hot, very uncomfortable, and, very bad tempered. For families heading to the coast, it must have been a wonderful start to their holidays.

Though bypassed now I still like to break my journeys in a now much quieter Tadcaster, with perhaps a visit to the gentleman's convenience, a sandwich, and a riverside walk to take in lungfuls of Taddy's distinctive air. If I've the time I like to go as far as the folly which stands as a perpetual monument to the hazards of the impetuous taking up of new technology. Built in 1846, the Virgin Bridge was completed by Hudson, the railway king of York, to carry a proposed new rail link between Leeds and York. Sadly for him, the booming railway industry over-reached itself, a financial crash ensued and no line was built. So this vanguard of the proposal has since sat astride the Wharfe, never achieving its purpose. However, it does now provide a superb platform to view the town, as well as link the two river banks for a pleasant circular tour.

Coxwold Church

This little treasure is almost hidden away at the foot of the Hambleton Hills, a mere handful of crow-flying miles from York. Photographically I found it interesting because the tower of the church is of a rare hexagonal design. But it is for its literary aspect that the place and nearby Shandy Hall really shine as a jewel in our heritage. For some time the Reverend Laurence Sterne was based in the area and it was here that he produced much of his work, in particular *Tristram Shandy*, later acknowledged by many to be the forerunner of the modern novel. In the hall itself there is an exquisite collection of Sterne first editions, thought to be the most comprehensive anywhere. In the churchyard lie Sterne's remains, though these were placed there quite recently. Indeed, that statement may be open to debate, as the remains are actually only assumed to be his. When the man originally died, his corpse was procured by the medical profession as an experimental cadaver, but it was recognized by one of the students who raised the alarm — sadly though, not before the tutorial was almost over. This included decapitation and there has always been some speculation as to whether the correct skull was returned with the rest of the body.

Talking of headless bodies, nearby Newburgh Priory is well worth a visit. Legend has it that through family ties the headless body of Oliver Cromwell found its last resting place in a sealed room somewhere within the walls. I say 'legend' because no member of the family will confirm the fact, nor will leave ever be given to attempt to discover the truth. Not even a member of the royal family was afforded that privilege; indeed Edward VII was scolded somewhat severely when he was caught trying to do so early this century.

WITHENS MOOR, HAWORTH

So much has been written, by far more eloquent and informed authors than I, about the Brontë sisters' love affair with the Moors, and the inspiration it gave them, that I was reluctant even to put finger to keyboard. Similarly, in photographic terms the area has been so saturated that I knew I would have difficulty in producing a new visual approach. However, it is such an important part of our heritage that I could find no reasonable excuse to omit it from my Yorkshire.

The exploitation is excessive with Brontë ices, Branwell cocktails, *Jane Eyre* salons – I kid you not, there is such a named hairdressing emporium! – and the like. However, the vast expanse of Moor means it is still possible to detach oneself totally from the commercialism, and experience the largely unchanged environment which inspired the exquisite poems and novels of the sisters. The one which immediately springs to mind is *Wuthering Heights,* for it is this book which seems most to epitomize the wild moody moorland, which for Emily embodied itself in the personality of Heathcliff. It's been a hobby of mine for some time, finding poems and passages from novels which include landscape description, and then visiting the locations to see if it is possible actually to feel the text. I've been to many locations all over the British Isles, most of which have been superbly conveyed by the authors' written words, but without any prejudice I can honestly say that to stand on this Moor, watching an oppressive sky cast a darkening cloak on the ruins of Top Withens, the weather-shattered boulders, and wind-flattened grasses, must rank as one of, if not *the,* most emotional. Try a walk yourself, and I'll guarantee that at some stage your ears will deceive your brain, and you'll swear that you can hear Cathy calling through the heather.

HELLIFIELD

Mention this place to thousands of travellers who have passed through it and they will recall one of the bleakest railway stations in the north. It also may be described as the beginning of the 'long drag' through Ribblesdale, then over the wild inhospitable Pennines to Carlisle. It is a line which can rival even the classic Scottish ones for grandeur.

Sadly, like many other remote stations, its bleak location is somewhat accentuated by neglect. Though I must admit that in some ways the decaying brick, rotting wood, rusting ironwork, and broken glass does help to provoke a heightened sense of nostalgia for the days of steam – days of grimy grinning stokers, soot-stained windows, uncomfortable seating and the choking smoky atmosphere of glowing coals. Looking along the windswept rain-splattered platform, you can almost hear the distant chug-chug-chug of the locomotive coming to save those stovepipe-hatted gents and crinolined ladies from the clutches of a cold northern winter's day. I hope British Rail don't take my wistful sentiments as a request and use it as an excuse to run their services down even further. It's one thing to imagine what the old days were like, but it's quite another to experience them first hand!

This platform has another very particular memory for me, of the time not too long ago when I was in an enviable position, which most boys and many men would have given anything to be in. I was photographing some new locomotive logos, and I had a complete goods train at my disposal. From here, several locations on an almost redundant branch line were to be used. This necessitated the whole caboodle being shunted backwards and forwards many times. To make life easier, from my sometimes distant camera point, I conversed with the driver by two-way radio. So, for a day, I had control of one of the biggest train sets in the world.

RIEVAULX ABBEY

These extensive remains regularly get a facial from a host of chisel and brush wielding beauty therapists, with the consequence that whilst always looking magnificent, to me they tend to be somewhat artificial. Having said that, I cannot deny that the ruins are extremely imposing, and remarkably complete. They boast excellent examples of early sewerage systems, chapels, living quarters and other necessities of a thriving community. At its zenith soon after its foundation in 1131, there were something like 140 monks and 600 lay brothers living within its walls. A small village, which with its flocks of animals and other concerns was undoubtedly self-sufficient.

Whatever I think about the restoration and commercialization of our ancient monuments, I cannot deny that the abbey must be among the grandest of Cistercian dwellings, and a thought-provoking must for anyone with a fertile imagination. I have often threaded my way around these great stone columns and tarried awhile under the roofless arches, trying to detect the faint ghostly echoes of the brothers in their silent devotions.

ROMAN ROAD, WHEELDALE MOOR

High on the moor above Goathland, lies the longest and best preserved example of Roman road in the British Isles. It probably originally stretched from Malton to one of the coastal signal stations, but this exposed stretch is the remains, the rest of it long disappeared amid the heather and bogs, or plundered for enclosure walls and the like. In fact what you see is only the foundations, because the top covering has likewise been recycled. But it has yielded secrets of engineering skills, and artifacts such as coins and pottery, giving today's archaeologists great insight into the lives of those Latin conquerors.

I've been on the road many times, because it's a popular local outing, and is crossed by the Lyke Wake Walk. However the most vivid memories it evokes are from the very first time I saw it. It was the first time I had been away from home, when the cub troop to which I belonged camped in the valley. I had mixed emotions, excitement at the trip, with its feeling of being grown-up, tempered by the dread of being in an alien environment without the security of nearest and dearest. I was about eight, and it would have been traumatic in any circumstances, but I contracted sickness and diarrhoea, and feeling so ill, all I really wanted was my mother, and even the head of the cub pack, Akela, lovely as she was, couldn't be a substitute. I remember it as the first really horrible time I'd experienced. On reflection, the horrible homesickness and pining I felt, must have been similar to that experienced by the young Legionnaires who tramped this road (though mine only lasted a week, and I was only a phone call away).

This is the only photograph of the set which has been manipulated slightly. I deliberately ensured there was no discernible sky, because I wanted the road to sweep through the frame as if to the past: you can easily imagine the hostile conditions here.

WHITE HORSE, KILBURN

'We're a proud race tha knows' and none of us likes to be bettered, especially not if it's by someone or something from outside the county. It's probably why we got this white horse. We didn't have one, but Southerners did, so the situation had to be rectified. Which was exactly what a local teacher and friends did in 1857, cutting out this figure whose vital statistics I won't bore you with, but if you and about fourteen friends want a picnic, and are prepared to expend surplus energy on a climb, then the eye of the creature will adequately accommodate you. Actually, as it turns out, the horse is also the product of a rare occurence for a Yorkshireman, a little bit of deception. Unfortunately, when cut, the underlying rock was too dark for real prominence at a distance, so a liberal covering of whitewash was regularly applied; more recently, whether caused by laziness or guilt, the whiteness was more permanently achieved by the laying of tons of chippings from the Yorkshire Wolds.

Every time I see this equine giant, it provides a reminder of the cardinal sin I, as a professional photographer, once committed: forgetting to carry my camera at all times. I'd been for a browse around the local workshops of the woodcarver Mousey Thompson, and afterwards decided on a brisk stroll up the bank to sit and contemplate the mechanical birds which soar effortlessly and silently on the thermal currents thereabouts. I thought I recognized the solitary man who was obviously of a similar mind, but ignoring him I eventually engaged in conversation with a very nice middle-aged lady. It was she who pointed him out as her son, up there to relax from the 'spot of bother' he was having. Suddenly, it dawned on me who he was: the central character in a sensational current courtroom drama. I could do nothing, but I often wonder if I would have intruded upon his privacy had I had my camera with me.

The postscript to the story unfolded that night. By chance I met a photographer friend from London days, who was retained by several national tabloids. Enquiring as to what brought him to my home town, he explained that he had been chasing the very character I had seen, who it was known had once resided in the area, hoping to show him relaxing from the pressures of his case, perhaps visiting old friends or stamping grounds. He was extremely frustrated at having missed such an advantageous lead over his contemporaries, as such an exclusive would have been worth a four or even five figure sum. I always carry a camera with me now!

JERVAULX ABBEY

These ruins are in extent comparable with many others of their type, but they are very much ruins – no attempt has been made to renovate, repair, or generally tart them up. The decaying weather-beaten archways, moss-encrusted stairways, and untamed plantlife which embraces every piece of stone it can, creates a relevant ambience in which to soak up history. Natural overgrowth and decomposition, for my money, provokes a far greater sense of the past than restored, yet sterile monuments. And really money is what it's down to: the owners of this abbey do not subject the visitor to astronomical entry fees, preferring instead to leave deposits in an honesty box to your discretion. The argument put forward for obligatory fees is the cost of upkeep, but quite honestly I feel that our heritage should be available to all, maintained out of the taxes we already pay, not viewed as a profitable enterprise! Neither should access be restricted.

These twelfth-century ruins are reputed to be the original factory of the succulent crumbly Wensleydale cheese, concocted by the monks here for their own consumption. After the forces of Henry VIII destroyed the abbey during the Dissolution, the secret recipe was passed to outside sources. Whether it was this Henry was really after, and the withholding of it was the treason, is not known, but Abbot Adam Sedburgh was imprisoned in the Tower of London, before being hanged at Tyburn. Perhaps the informer, of whatever the crime, was an 'ex'-monk, aggrieved at being expelled for over-curdling the milk!

DRUIDS' TEMPLE, NEAR MASHAM

A folly, according to the *Oxford English Dictionary* is 'a costly structure considered useless or otherwise foolish'. Consequently, it tends to be used to describe anything which, in the eyes of the Establishment, does not conform to its rules of utility. One or two of their own creations might perhaps be eligible for such a title! Literally speaking no building should be so labelled because regardless of how eccentric it may appear, it must have served some purpose to the perpetrator.

Such is the case with this temple, created by one William Danby. It may have been that it was his attempt, though slightly more peculiar than others, to adhere to the estate improvement fad of the time, or it may have been to provide work in an area which had a high rate of unemployment (labourers were paid a shilling a day for their time). In either case, it was useful, and was surely no folly. Whatever the reasons behind its design and inception, Druids' Temple remains the most complete of its kind in the United Kingdom. Reputed to have been fashioned on Stonehenge plans, it is in fact elliptical, and has an extra chamber at one end, now home to a rare luminous lichen. When a place resembles an ancient temple, there are invariably going to be rumours of mystical ceremonies and witchcraft, and this proves no exception. Whilst none of these rumours, including the one that it was for this that Danby originally created it, can be substantiated, I did wonder if the charred logs in the foreground really were the remnants of a Scout camp fire! Never mind the weird atmosphere, or the markings on certain stones such as the altar table. . . .

HARROGATE

It's amazing how we tend to imagine that the worse something tastes, then the better it must be for our health – cod liver oil being a perfect example. The renowned female traveller Celia Fiennes on a visit to this area in the seventeenth century, commented that 'there is the Sulpher or Stincking Spaw, not improperly term'd for the Smell being so very strong and offensive that I could not force my horse near the Well'. It therefore comes as no surprise that Harrogate grew in popularity as a health resort. 'Taking the waters' probably reached a peak during the nineteenth century when as many as nineteen coaches a day ran here from various parts of the country, in addition to the personal coaches and chaises of the really wealthy. Consequently much of Harrogate's architecture is splendidly Victorian, worthy of at least a short wander through.

Even after the vogue for quaffing the vile-tasting waters declined, the town was still a focal point for many; a genteel resort for the moneyed classes whilst employees clattered off to the seaside. It was probably then that the gardens came into their own as a place to stroll amidst exotic plant life, partake of refreshment on wrought-iron terraces, or simply take in the sun seated at one of the many colonnades, before retiring to the town to participate in one of the regular tea-dances. A rest-cure vacation from the pressures of the world or perhaps a place to become lost in for a time. It was here that Agatha Christie was eventually found after her celebrated disappearance.

My favourite part of Harrogate is these gardens, which at times seem very distant from the 'real' world. Caught in time they have steadfastly refused to keep pace with the twentieth century, preferring to lag nostalgically in the town's halcyon days, when landaus were driven in the park, and gentlefolk were propelled at dignified speed in bath chairs. A last remnant of the Empire's days.

KNARESBOROUGH

As evening descends over the River Nidd, spanned by its magnificent railway viaduct, the lights of Knaresborough appear in the houses. Built up the hillside as it is, I always find the town's appearance more than a little reminiscent of a Cornish fishing village. Steeped in darkness now are the castle ruins, and the Chapel of Our Lady of the Crag cut deep into the rock. The shops are closing down for the night, including the chemist's, in the market square, which claims to be the oldest in England. Perhaps now we should venture down that right bank of the river, so near to habitation, and yet. . . .

Not even moonlight penetrates the thick tangle of branches above. The undergrowth through which we stumble is of the blackest hue, and yet still produces mere hints of shadows to dance across the path. And then suddenly the forest parts, no more do the leaves brush across our faces, sending cold shivers down our spines. Before us a luminous spectacle beckons. Slowly, fearfully, we approach this altar of decadence, which is adorned by the gifts of subservient followers, prepared to pay homage to the force of . . . Just a minute. A cricket bat, a teddy bear, a naughty item from an Anne Summers' lingerie party, what kind of offerings are these? I mean they're not even the real thing. Solid stone, every one. Actually they were once the real thing, yes even the last-named, because this is the famous Dropping Well. If you leave an item suspended so that the water flows over it, the limestone in the water will eventually turn it into a stone carving. The effect is just like stalactites and stalagmites.

So, you see, it's all easily explained naturally, even if it is also purported to have been the home of the fifteenth-century prophetess Mother Shipton – she who forecast the coming of metal birds, horseless carriages and the like centuries before they were invented.

YORK MINSTER

Sometimes each of us must stand accused of taking our environment for granted, and being blissfully ignorant of some of the treasures stored therein. I am occasionally blatantly guilty of this offence, and in no way is this more obvious than in the case of the city of York. I have to admit that though it is the city for which my county is named, culturally it has remained largely unexplored on my part. I have never made a point of meandering in and out of the walls, soaking in the charm which has successively attracted Saxon, Roman, Viking, American and Far Eastern invaders, though thankfully in the cases of the latter two, the only plundering perpetrated is of the souvenir shops; nor have I investigated the history left by the earlier ones. Whilst I am familiar with some of the more interesting little quirks of the city, I have never pursued them with the vigour awarded to certain other areas within this book, so even though I know that Dick Turpin is buried within its walls I am ashamed to say that I am unaware of the actual site of his resting place. However I *do* know where Guy Fawkes received the education which brought him to the quite sensible solution of destroying a parliament, for as a lad I was regularly engaged in tribal warfare with more recent pupils of St Peter's School.

Inevitably, of all the twenty-plus churches which ooze architectural and historical interest, and the many other buildings and sites which should not be missed by any visitor, the most famous and photogenic is York Minster. In providing the illustration for this, through a low night shot, I have tried to break free from the more normal tourist image and hopefully show some of the romantic character of this building which rises from the skyline of the city overshadowing and dominating all else.

Busby Stoop Inn

Often, I think, the essence of an area is reflected in, or perhaps even created by, its old tales, so wherever I travel I make a point of keeping my ears open for such, especially if, as in this case, research means spending some time in the sport of elbow-bending and lip-wetting. Though the inn was added after the crossroads here was so named, I do, as this picture shows, like the sense of humour of the landlord. Busby himself was apparently a bit of a rogue who had the misfortune to be caught. He was hung in chains at the crossroads as a deterrent to others.

The story about the inn that I particularly like is of the death chair. It seems that the seat in question was used by a slightly cantankerous old local, who always became agitated if he arrived to find someone else availing themselves of its comforts. He probably spent so much on ale in his time that he felt he'd purchased the exclusive rights to it! After his death, strange, and sometimes serious accidents befell any who used it. Whilst it is possible that this was a series of coincidences, they were enough to convince the locals that it might possibly be cursed, and consequently it was always left empty. Thankfully, it has now been stored so there's no need to stare apprehensively at each seat should you happen to patronize this establishment.

BRIMHAM ROCKS

In 1869, a gentleman by the name of Mackintosh put forward a theory, supported by vast amounts of 'evidence', that the landforms of England were moulded by the action of the ocean. His theory suggested that Brimham rocks were actually marine stacks eroded by the sea, and he termed them 'insular wrecks'. I prefer the notion that they have been and still are being carved by Mother Nature the sculptress, using tools of wind and rain. Many of them have been given evocative names, such as Dancing Bear and The Pulpit, by equally romantic souls. This area between Ripon and Pateley Bridge is awe-inspiring to all who visit, and it is said that the rocks were a profound influence on the young Henry Moore, helping to stylize his early work.

Whenever I visit, I feel that there is something mystical and indeed threatening about the place; no more so than one cold February morning when I arrived to catch a sunrise. There I was at 5 a.m., snow at my feet, and a hot coffee in my hand, hoping for a fiery backdrop against which these majestic sculptures could be silhouetted. The atmosphere was eerie, every awakening bird reaching for the sky in search of an early morning feed, every scurrying small furry creature escaping those very piercing eyes, every sway of leafless branches in the biting wind, sent shivers down my spine, and caused a tensing of muscle, until by the time the sun did paint the sky in a myriad of violent hues I was glad that I'd brought a tripod for my camera – I shook too much to hold it steady! Though this is how I find the stones and their environs, a folk tale portrays them in a more romantic light. It begins in the usual way, boy and girl fall in love, but he is a poor farmer's son, and she is the rich squire's daughter. The romance is forbidden so they run away, and shelter from her pursuing father overnight beneath the rock. Morning comes and they are discovered, but deciding they would rather die than be parted, they climb the rock, and in a suicide pact both jump. Fortunately, she has on a large skirt and a mass of petticoats which act as a parachute, allowing the terrified couple to float gently to earth. From a distance, and through a mist of anger, alcohol, bad eyesight, or a combination of all three, the squire imagines that the billowing clothes are actually angels, who, refusing to let the couple die, have lowered them safely. Believing that marriage is made in heaven and that this is a sign, the squire relents and they live happily ever after.

St Michel du Monte

This church is a constant reminder of how I obviously don't always follow the advice I give when lecturing on photography: always to keep one's eyes open and continually to observe the surroundings. It stands very prominently on a hill quite near to Fountains Abbey, and yet I failed to notice it for some time on my travels! However, this has been rectified numerous times since, during all seasons. It provides a wealth of different perspectives, especially when viewed using the fallen and standing trees as a foreground. It also offers the prospect of a spectacular panorama on a clear day.

Originally mentioned as Erlesholt in the 'Domesday Book', traces of ramparts and a burial ground suggest that the hill was occupied many centuries prior to this. The first chapel was erected about 1200, probably for the convenience of pilgrims and the Fountains monks working the fields; but this structure dates only from 1718. It was built at the instigation of John Aislabie, who was responsible for the planning and construction of the massive complex of lakes, temples and canals on the nearby estate of Studley Royal. Among the archives there is a joinery bill relating to work done here, which includes repair to gaming tables. An intriguing item for a church, though, come to think of it, if the religious orders disapproved and actively discouraged wagering, what better cover for an illegal casino!

How Stean Gorge

If I'm honest, then there is very little to write about this place. It's one of those locations where I go because of what there is to see, and for no other reason. Even though the enterprising owners will relieve you of one of those annoying golden coins for admission. However, the entrance fee is well worth it. Here, one can sit and watch the infant Nidd, before she grows into a relatively boring river, enlarge her artistic mark, as she continues her eternal sculpturing of the rocky gorge. I'm a little confused though why it has gained the nickname of Little Switzerland; I would have thought that Little Grand Canyon was more appropriate. Anyway, whichever you think it resembles doesn't really matter, I like the place because of the many interesting shapes the water has created, all of which make excellent camera fodder.

GRASSINGTON

A 'Bed and Breakfast' sign is a common sight in the Dales, as everyone seems to dabble in it to a certain degree, whatever the size of their abode. It brings in some extra income, and helps alleviate the shortage of accommodation. It still seems to be on the increase though, which I think is no bad thing, as the search for suitable accommodation is part of the fun of a touring holiday. Anyway, how would our countryside look if massive modern plastic 'n' glass hotels began sprouting behind every stone wall, or beneath every crag? Though if the megalomaniac leisure tycoons have their way, the 'village' capable of handling three thousand tourists a day being proposed to desecrate green fields near the Bedale end of Wensleydale will only be the forerunner of many. Such grandiose schemes *must* be thwarted at the outset!

Grassington has, through necessity, succumbed to catering for the tourist industry by the provision of memento and food establishments of a very high standard, whilst managing to retain its dignity. The charm of the cobbled market square, from which radiates the 'folds' or alleys, narrow enough to be mildly claustrophobic yet picturesque in their close construction, makes this a fascinating place to explore. Its situation meant it had long been a centre for trading, but much of the present town was built to accommodate the influx of Welsh and Cornish miners in the eighteenth and nineteenth centuries to work the rich lead seams still traceable even now above the town. Even when it's thronging with tourists there is still an air of leisurely dignity here, making it difficult to believe how violent, lawless, and insanitary the community became during these times. Indeed, until the arrival of religious reformers, observers could be forgiven for imagining they were at the centre of the Klondike gold rush, instead of the Yorkshire Dales.

SHEEP

Sheep are indigenous to the whole of Yorkshire, yet are associated most particularly with the Yorkshire Dales and Moors, in much the same way as deer are linked with Scotland. If you travelled elsewhere and didn't see any ovine mammals you wouldn't worry, but if you failed to see any here you'd certainly feel cheated! Much of our county is only suitable for the rearing of these creatures, something which has become a fine art among many hill farmers; as it was with the monks before them. I suppose the ancestors of those we see now could be regarded as having been responsible for the growth of the wool industry of West Yorkshire. They have a distinct fascination for me, so I felt no folio would be complete without at least one study.

I am generally very ignorant about the characters of the animals, and in being so, gullible. So that when I once inquired why one, having given birth, was shuffling around on bent front legs, I actually believed the reply that the illusion of going downhill made it run faster! Seriously, though, they amuse and intrigue me because their basic characteristics are quite contradictory. On the one hand, I find them inquisitive, so that if I'm in one place photographing for any length of time, it is inevitable that at least one will venture closer to observe my actions; yet any sudden movement will bring their timidity to the fore and they'll go scooting off rapidly. I wrote *they*, because that's another trait I've discovered. They really are very gregarious, so that if I can work without startling the initially curious one, then the others will soon follow, like humans! Photographing them was a problem though, for even when working to a gallery of the nosy, every movement of the camera towards them initiated a stampede. Either as a breed they are modest retiring folk not given to posing for portraits, or else my body odour must closely resemble the smell of mint sauce!

Despairing I was, until this flock showed a vague willingness to hang around. After some straight talking – for I knew I wouldn't be able to pull the wool over their eyes – they consented to one shot and a brief biography for posterity! The family gathering is Baasil and Baabara who've been married for several years, and the little jumpers are their second lot of Baabies.

KILNSEY CRAG

Chiang Lee, a Silent traveller in the Dales, once likened this crag the slowly sliding glacier forgot to the enormous stone animals adorning the Ming Emperors' tomb at Nanking. I must admit the great overhanging top gives it an air of threatening menace, making anyone immediately below thankful that the rest of the scar prevents it from toppling onto them. Nevertheless, I find it rather exciting to sit beneath the massive bulk, which overlooks the internationally-famous Kilnsey sheepdog trials and wall-building competitions. Usually I can be a spectator to some rock climber attempting to scale its limestone wall, which it has long been a challenge to conquer – probably because one stage in the climb requires a horizontal body, extremely strong digital extremities to curl into available fissures, and steel nerves: qualities found only in the most accomplished exponents of the sport. Indeed, it remained unbeaten until the 1950s when the advent of modern accessories assisted the feat.

The acute overhang also creates the illusion of the crag seeming to be much nearer to jaunty motorists than it actually is; consequently the recently-evolved pastime of trying to hit the rock face with stones thrown from the road proves in practice to be almost impossible. I have tried on several occasions and failed miserably, but that could be because of my puny physique!

ARNCLIFFE, YORKSHIRE DALES

The real name of this place is Amerdale, which Yorkshire's own enterprising television company corrupted into Emmerdale for its long-running series. Indeed, in the early stages scenes in 'Beckindale' were filmed here, and the inn on the green was temporarily renamed The Woolpack. I understand from one of the cast that the very first shots caused more than a little consternation to passing motorists. Well, how were they to know that the crowd standing around a hearse having a quick cigarette were only actors waiting for another 'take' of Jacob Sugden's last ride, and not actually irreverent mourners?

Perhaps it's this connection which endears me to the village, for there have been many times of homesickness when the series has cheered me up with reminders of 'real' life in Yorkshire; or it could be that the whole essence of a way of life in which I would love to participate can be summed up by that Post Office tucked away in the corner.

GORDALE SCAR

This great gorge is reckoned to have once been a cave whose roof fell in and its awesome presence has for centuries been a must on the itinerary of any passing traveller. Some notable ones have even made special excursions, just to experience the dark perpendicular walls which overhang so much as to almost blot out the sky. Consequently it has been described in countless journals and poems and it has similarly acted as a magnet to many artists both professional and amateur, numbered among whom was the legendary J.M.W. Turner.

For all this, nothing can adequately prepare you for the impact of a first visit. Your gentle stroll through a mildly sloping valley is suddenly cut short by a mighty dark chasm yawning before you. Its dank grey walls tower high over you; the sounds of falling water echo and re-echo until they become a mighty roar. To stare at the gnarled rock amidst all this is to imagine an age when sabre-toothed tigers and mammoths ruled the earth. If you're lucky you may even catch a glimpse of a strangely stooping hairy creature bellowing fearful grunts as you ascend the cataract which provides the only through passage in the do. If you do, then don't forget to say 'hello', because I quite enjoy entering into civilized conversation while I sit and soak in the mystical atmosphere of the place.

MALHAM COVE

We've trod the path which a mighty geological upheaval created many ages ago, but our way is barred by a barrier which resisted these forces of nature. Above us is a mighty cove, its sheer walls of limestone towering hundreds of feet above us. Now we either retrace our steps, or make a long detour to follow the remainder of Malhamdale, unless of course you fancy following that chap in the top right of the picture. Though I think that route may be only for human flys with nerves of steel – else, one wrong foothold could send you bumping and grinding down its wall just like Tom. For it was on a visit here, from his temporary residence at Malham Tarn, that Charles Kingsley looking out from the top, remarked that the natural black streaks in the rock were like a coal dust trail a dirty little chimney sweep's apprentice might have left, had he tumbled down the face. And thus was born an idea that was later expanded to become *The Water-Babies*.

Whilst the cove inspired a classic children's novel, it also provides a mystery which has never been completely solved. Once a river ran from the tarn and crashed over the cove to where we now stand, but due to the effect of water erosion on the soluble limestone the river eventually disappeared at a place now called, for obvious reasons, Water Sinks, to continue its course underground. Emerging, one would imagine, at the bottom of the cove? Not so, for as modern chemical tests have proved, it actually emerges several miles down the valley, and the stream that emerges here is totally unconnected. But where it does come from is one of Nature's mysteries, the solution to which she has no intention of divulging.

SEMERWATER

One of my recurring observations is how outsiders view us Yorkshire persons, and our environment. This ranges from the fantasy that we all wear cloth caps, shine up cobbled streets with wooden clogs on our feet, wander round muttering ''Eee by gum lad tha' knows', to the illusion that we are rude, insular, unsociable, ignorant, arrogant, with an obsessive love of our county. Not true; visitors are astounded to find us friendly, amenable, and more than willing to share our perfections with lesser mortals!

Our forefathers learned painfully, that the rewards of fraternity are infinitely preferable to those of enmity; and this was the lesson of Semerwater. Here in Wensleydale there was once a great trading centre, which eventually became filled with unscrupulous greedy merchants. A passing angel, tired and hungry, entered the city searching for food and shelter, but because he had no money, he was turned away, often none too politely, from every door at which he enquired. Exhausted, cold and disillusioned, he made his way out of the town and climbed slowly up the hillside. About half-way up he came upon a ramshackle hut which belonged to a poor shepherd. The shepherd and his wife, seeing the angel, took pity on him, offering him a bed for the night, and a share of what little food they had. This restored the angel's faith in human nature, but even so he decided that the city dwellers should be taught a lesson, and before retiring he called upon the elements to mete out justice.

When the shepherd and his wife awoke the following morning the angel had gone, and so had the city. In its place was the lake of Semerwater, by the shore two great stones bearing the gouge marks left by the fingers of inhabitants as they desperately tried to save themselves from the flood. Since then the dark foreboding waters of the lake, from the depths of which occasionally emanates the ghostly peal of repentant bells, have provided a constant reminder of the consequences which lack of phil-anthropism brings.

AYSGARTH FALLS

In recent summers, the word 'falls' has been a bit of a misnomer – 'trickles' would probably be more apt. Still, at least they haven't dried up completely yet. Here, they are a series of steps rather than deeply plunging cascades, but when the River Ure is in full spate they are a magnificent sight. The vast volumes of water which then gush and swirl tempestuously over the rocks do so with a roar which can sometimes be heard several miles away.

I remember photographing the falls once at such a time, when not only was the dry foreground a violent whirlpool, but also if I'd tried to stand where I did for this picture, I would have been swept away by the torrent. Sadly, its seems that such a spectacle has not occurred at all this year, to the disappointment of the many who have visited.

OLD GANG MINES

There are all sorts of remnants dotted about the Dales having either direct or indirect connection with Yorkshire's eras of mining: hamlets where the workers resided, old tracks on which they trudged to and from employment, and the remains of mines and the ore smelting mills themselves. This is perhaps the most complete reminder of those days. Nearby are also the levels through which the seams were reached.

I did once venture a short way into one of the latter – *only* a short way, because my natural yellow streak glowed brighter as the narrow passage darkened. As soon as it curved enough for the entrance to be obscured that was enough for me to turn tail. Perhaps noticing that the passage walls were composed of very neat brickwork without any visible cement was also a persuader. I'm told that on one such level I could actually have progressed through some flooding to the remains of an engine room. Being told about it is as far as I intend to pursue the matter though!

Care must be taken when exploring these old areas, because many of the shafts are not adequately sealed and the edges, particularly of the vertical ones, are somewhat eroded.

RICHMOND

Watch the Swale as it weaves its way around the town, forming the valley which the castle was built to protect. The castle, the oldest and largest military structure of its kind in the United Kingdom, must have provided an excellent deterrent, for since it was built in Norman times it has never seen action. Now it rests serenely as one of the town's major attractions, along with the Georgian theatre dating from 1788, and the curious Church of the Holy Trinity, under the north aisle of which were once shops, now the headquarters and museum of the Green Howards.

Its place above the gentle flow of the river implies that it sleeps placidly now, redundant, resigned to a future of curiosity. But perhaps not, for beneath its battlements lie, it is rumoured, King Arthur and his Knights, merely resting lest the shores of Britain are again invaded, when they will awake to defend the Sceptred Isle. It may be legend, though there is a record of a workman who, lost in the maze of underground passages, came upon them after breaking down a wall. He eventually found his way out into the open but sadly was never able to lead anyone back to the chamber. This might be taken as Yorkshire imagination, but surely it could be true. The passages must exist, for was it not one of these which connected the Castle with Easby Abbey? The one through which a drummer boy was ordered to march and beat his drum, so that those above could follow the sound and establish its path, and from which he never emerged? If you doubt my word, one day lend the soil hereabouts your ear. Then when you hear the rat-a-tat-tat echoing from far below. . . .

GUNNERSIDE

Now will you look at that? Doesn't it just epitomize most people's idea of a typical Dales scene? Fields with a few sheep and cows, quaint little barns stuffed full of hay, and rough meandering hand-built stone walls.

Though I'm not ashamed to admit it, its my image of the Dales too. It's part of the attraction of the national park, and one of the reasons that I so often find myself tramping the paths around here. It's great when I can lose myself amongst the rural pleasures of the Dales, idling the highways and byways, with barely a thought for the rigours of photographic employment. Unfortunately, its capacity for continually presenting refreshing new overtones, even to a very familiar contour, is such that on those rare occasions when I have deliberately forgotten my trade tools, I have instantly regretted the decision and become an unbearable companion with whom to while away the journey!

Window and Wall, High Dales

Once in a while I may be wandering around a place, when suddenly a subject will catch my eye. It may not be the most exciting there is, it may not seem to have any relevance to the reason which had brought me there. It may even at the time appear to be the total opposite of what I am searching for. And yet, inexplicably, it will draw me in and persuade me to loose off a few frames and dally with different perspectives or compositions.

Such was the case here. The autopilot just seemed to engage. It's not any particular location, and I don't know whether it belongs to a farm, a cottage, or an old storehouse. I suspect that my sub-conscious insisted on the shot being taken to illustrate one of my dreams – to find a hideaway of just such a vintage, restore it and then spend my days writing, taking photographs and occasionally leading photographic walking classes. Dreams are wonderful things to escape to, though have you noticed they never touch on such mundane subjects as money, and the means to support such an ideal existence?

DALES FARM SCENE

The photograph on page 126 was of a general agricultural scene which could be repeated over many of the Dales. This is one which might be seen along the single track roads which meander among and infiltrate the rural charms.

I was particularly drawn to this because of the tractor. Look at the number plate, its pre-single letter registration. It must be at least twenty-eight years old! That must make it a candidate for an antiques auction. But isn't it a glamorous old beast, its advanced state of dilapidation and collection of work scars serving only to accentuate its appeal. I bet it still starts first time too.

When I come across old machines like this, it makes me think about how much farming has progressed. There again, all those time-saving gargantuans I see cutting a swathe through the vast cornfields on the plains would be little use in the relatively minute enclosed pastures that the undulating folds of the land reluctantly permit around here. Though relatively few farms practise agriculture, most preferring livestock. I was talking to one farmer recently who, though only fifty years old, remembers as a child having to harvest in the old style – scything, gathering and stooking by hand, then turning the crop at regular intervals over a period of days, to allow the wind to penetrate and dry it. Even then the graft was not finished, for it had to be threshed, and baled. As he sat astride his combine, watching the baler following behind, he, for one, was more than a mite thankful that some of the burdens have now been relieved by technological progress.

BUTTERTUBS PASS

I don't know exactly what you expected here – probably the same as me, when I was first taken to see Buttertubs by my parents. The very name conjured up childish images of an endless pass lined with great casks. To say I was disappointed was an understatement, as not only were they sunk into the ground and therefore not immediately visible, but also they only stretch for a few dozen yards, if that. I soon overcame my despondency with bravery, though, as I dared to peer over the rims of the shafts into their dark depths, which were reputed to be bottomless, and indeed, according to some locals, deeper even than that.

Uncle Albert was with us, and, being a bit of a joker, took it upon himself to disappear into one. I began to panic, thinking he was falling towards Australia, and that I would never see him again. But before long his hiding place was given away by tell tale spirals of smoke from his pipe, rising from the bowels of the earth. So I discovered that they were not actually bottomless at all!

Many of the buttertubs are not very deep, but they are nevertheless an interesting phenomenon, and in recent times one or two new earthquake-like cracks have appeared. It is rumoured that their name came about because farmers used their cold depths to store unsold butter, until the following day's market. I find them at their most interesting after heavy rain, when the limestone takes on a fluorescent but treacherous sheen, and a myriad of tiny waterfalls cascade onto the pot floors, in a magnified echoing grumble.

HARDRAW FORCE

The way to the waterfall here is barred by the Green Dragon, a very difficult obstacle to negotiate. Though because this guardian of the path is a convivial hostelry, the danger is of being soaked on the inside, not fried on the outside!

At the entrance to its valley, where its sides are still gentle enough to scramble up, there is an old bandstand where concerts were once held. They attracted the best of the West Yorkshire colliery bands and large appreciative audiences who would seat themselves on the natural ledges up the grass bank. Happily there are attempts to revive this traditional bank holiday pastime.

Beyond this, the walls of the valley become sheer and afforested, so that even on the best days the sun rarely filters in to warm the rocks. At the end it widens out into a basin, the walls of which, after centuries of erosion, have become concave so that now the top protrudes beyond the bottom. As the great column of water flows over this, plummeting into the middle of the deep pool below, it is now possible to walk right round behind the Force. When our winters were colder it used to freeze into a vast icicle, and daring souls would scale it, as they might a Swiss glacier.

Perhaps it's the combination of the continuous roar of the water, the oppressively close walls, and the fine misty spray, which creates the ethereal atmosphere. I am often unnerved by a sense that, especially at twilight, I am being observed here by trolls and hobgoblins, perched, legs dangling wickedly over the rim of this great amphitheatre, as they chatter and laugh in evil high-pitched excitement. Yet its magical, almost supernatural magnetism continually draws me back to linger here in their secret court.

RIBBLEHEAD VIADUCT

It is inconceivable that any tour of Yorkshire should miss out this lasting memorial to the pioneers who built our railways – and by that I mean the navvies not the planners! Who, between 1869 and 1876 endured atrocious conditions in order to lay a track across some of the most inhospitable landscape in the British Isles. A feat of engineering which not only included building this viaduct, but also tunnelling under Blea Moor. Many of the men had their families with them, living in a temporary shanty town hereabouts. The route was hailed as a brilliant success when it was opened, and created a faster line to Carlisle, in addition to providing a service to isolated local communities en route. But at what a cost – in human misery and suffering, rather than pounds, shillings and pence. In nearby Chapel-le-Dale, the church of St Leonards has a sad marble slab commemorating the result of the greed of the railway barons: two hundred men, women and children who succumbed to the constant deprivation and harsh winters.

The journey across Ribblehead is breathtaking to make, and because it's a continuous incline, the engine will always have a full head of steam belching from the funnel. Quite a stirring sight, especially in the winters of yore when it was apparently not uncommon to have to plough the line free of snow! The fact that we can make this journey at all, and that it can introduce the younger generation to the acrid smoke and red-hot cinder sparks of coal-fired propulsion is due to the stubborn determination of the local population. For, when British Rail declared that the route was not economically viable, and so it would be closed, they opposed the plans with a campaign of military precision, informing and gaining the support of the public in general, and the railway enthusiast in particular. The petitions, protests, and public outrage succeeded admirably, and eventually caused the management of the lumbering giant to rescind its decision. The 'irreparable' viaduct was made safe, and to attract a lucrative tourist trade, steam was re-introduced.

I can only vaguely remember the original end of steam, but my one really vivid recollection is of the driver's handbag. What secrets were contained in this sinister leather package which was regularly exchanged between driver and station master? My childhood illusions were somewhat shattered in later life when I discovered that it was nothing more than the single line key, to ensure that no trains would meet head on along such tracks!

BELOW INGLEBOROUGH

This is the second largest abundance of limestone pavement in the British Isles. Now it's not often you will hear a Yorkshireman admit to anything in his county not being the best, but, unfortunately, in this case, having visited The Burren in Ireland, I know it to be an undisputed fact. But at least there's nowhere quite like it in the UK! The miniature grand canyons are called grykes, and are formed by acid rainwater eating into the limestone. The bits missed, which can be used as precarious stepping-stones, are called clints. Tread warily when wet, as, as I know only too well from painful experience, it is all too easy to slip and jam a foot in a fissure.

Except for a few stunted trees, barely seeming to survive, it looks barren. A false impression, because the grykes provide excellent conditions for all manner of small plants, some of which are rare, and consequently it's quite a botanist's paradise. As you would imagine from looking at the surface here, below here is also a maze of canyons, with roofs though. The easy way to explore these is in the commercially-created cavern walks; the hard, more dangerous way is by potholing. Only once was I persuaded to engage in the latter, and I spent the whole trip extremely frightened, and in spite of having the proper equipment, very, very cold, especially when immersed in the underground waters.

Ahead of this is Ingleborough itself, once thought to be the highest mountain in Britain, though we now know that it can't even claim the right to Yorkshire's crown. On its summit there are hut circle remains, with a massive stone battlement around the plateau's edge. These originate from the Iron Age, but the mystery of who fortified this bleak mountain, and why, endures. Considering its solitude and impregnability, whoever used the settlement obviously needed to defend themselves from someone. But *who* posed an interruption to their peaceful existence? A prehistoric tax inspector perhaps?

PENDRAGON

And so we come to the end of the journey. Where to close was no problem, and while it happens to be Pendragon Castle, reputedly assembled by King Arthur's uncle, it could have been anywhere the sun sets.

You will have noticed the absence, bar the one exception for dramatic purposes, of any human element in the photographs. That's because I believe it's the environment, history, and heritage of Yorkshire which create pride within its people. When we who sustain that pride today, have, like the sun, sunk into dark oblivion, that which we now hold dear will still remain. Reminders of the past, both good and bad, the foundation with which to educate, and imbue Yorkshire pride in future generations.

PHOTOGRAPHIC NOTES

I've included this technical data in case it may be of interest, although I realize that to many of you the numbers and figures will be as understandable as the hieroglyphics on an Egyptian tomb.

The cameras and lenses used were as recorded. The films used were Ilford FP4 in the medium format camera, rated at 100 ASA but processed as per standard times given in the leaflets. In the 35 mm I used Ilford XP1. When this latter film was first introduced I admit that I treated it with some scepticism. A film which could be rated from 200 to 1600 ASA on the same roll and then processed in C41 colour chemicals. . . . Who were they kidding! I would now like to make a written apology to that company's boffins for doubting their genius. I rated it at 200 ASA, and had it processed through a local High Street processing laboratory. I hand-printed the originals on Ilford Multigrade paper and made only one of each before destroying the negative. In this way, if anyone wishes to buy the originals they know that the market will never be flooded with copies.

At no time did I, nor do I ever use filters in either my monochrome or colour work. I detest the use of such artificial aids, and believe the use of them portrays a creature who not only has the audacity grievously to insult Mother Nature by believing they could improve upon her creative talents, but also shows that they lack the most important thing a landscape photographer can have – patience.

TECHNICAL DATA

MAP NO.	TITLE	CAMERA	LENS	SPEED	STOP
1	NORTH YORKSHIRE MOORS	BRONICA S2A	75 MM	1/30	F11
2	GRAVESTONE, LEEDS	NIKON FA	24 MM	1/60	F16
3	FARNDALE	NIKON FA	24 MM	1/8	F22
4	NORTH YORKSHIRE MOORS	NIKON FA	24 MM	1/30	F16
5	GLAISDALE PACK BRIDGE	NIKON FA	50 MM	1/250	F16
6	ROSEBERRY TOPPING	BRONICA S2A	75 MM	1/60	F22
7	WAINSTONES	BRONICA S2A	75 MM	1/4	F22
8	MIDDLESBROUGH TRANSPORTER BRIDGE	BRONICA S2A	75 MM	1/250	F11
9	TEESSIDE	NIKON FA	50 MM	1/250	F11
10	NORTH SEA FISHING BOAT	NIKON FA	500 MM	1/2000	F8
11	REDCAR	NIKON FA	200 MM	1/250	F11
12	SALTBURN	BRONICA S2A	75 MM	1/125	F16
13	BOULBY CLIFFS	NIKON FA	24 MM	1/250	F22
14	KETTLENESS	NIKON FA	24 MM	1/250	F22
15	STAITHES	NIKON FA	50 MM	1/250	F11
16	WHITBY HARBOUR	BRONICA S2A	75 MM	1/15	F11
17	ROBIN HOOD'S BAY	BRONICA S2A	75 MM	1/15	F16
18	SCARBOROUGH HARBOUR	BRONICA S2A	75 MM	1/60	F22
19	CAYTON BAY	BRONICA S2A	75 MM	1/30	F16
20	FILEY BRIGG	NIKON FA	24 MM	1/125	F11
21	FLAMBOROUGH HEAD	NIKON FA	50 MM	1/250	F11
22	RUDSTON	NIKON FA	24 MM	1/60	F22
23	BEVERLEY MINSTER	NIKON FA	24 MM	2 SECS	F32
24	SPURN POINT	NIKON FA	24 MM	1/500	F11
25	STONE CREEK, HUMBER ESTUARY	NIKON FA	24 MM	1/1000	F8
26	CITY CENTRE, HULL	BRONICA S2A	75 MM	1/250	F8
27	FERRYBRIDGE	BRONICA S2A	75 MM	1/125	F11
28	FITZWILLIAM	BRONICA S2A	75 MM	1/4	F22
29	PIT HEAD, BARNSLEY	BRONICA S2A	75 MM	1/60	F22
30	HEPTONSTALL	NIKON	24 MM	1/60	F32
31	ORPHANS' GRAVE	NIKON FA	24 MM	1/250	F16
32	DWELLING, CALDERDALE	NIKON FA	50 MM	1/60	F16
33	SALTAIRE	NIKON FA	50 MM	1/30	F11
34	COW AND CALF ROCKS, ILKLEY MOOR	BRONICA S2A	75 MM	1/15	F22
35	LEEDS MILL	NIKON FA	24 MM	1/8	F22
36	LEEDS–LIVERPOOL CANAL	BRONICA S2A	75 MM	1/125	F11
37	VIRGIN BRIDGE, TADCASTER	NIKON FA	50 MM	1/250	F11
38	COXWOLD CHURCH	BRONICA S2A	75 MM	1/30	F22

MAP NO.	TITLE	CAMERA	LENS	SPEED	STOP
39	WITHENS MOOR, HAWORTH	NIKON FA	24 MM	1/15	F16
40	HELLIFIELD	BRONICA S2A	75 MM	1/30	F11
41	RIEVAULX ABBEY	NIKON FA	24 MM	1/60	F22
42	ROMAN ROAD, WHEELDALE MOOR	NIKON FA	24 MM	1/30	F32
43	WHITE HORSE, KILBURN	BRONICA S2A	75 MM	1/60	F16
44	JERVAULX ABBEY	BRONICA S2A	75 MM	1/60	F11
45	DRUIDS' TEMPLE, NEAR MASHAM	NIKON FA	24 MM	1/60	F32
46	HARROGATE	NIKON FA	50 MM	1/250	F16
47	KNARESBOROUGH	NIKON FA	24 MM	1/60	F11
48	YORK MINSTER	NIKON FA	24 MM	30 SECS	F32
49	BUSBY STOOP INN	NIKON FA	50 MM	1/500	F11
50	BRIMHAM ROCKS	NIKON FA	24 MM	1/125	F16
51	ST MICHEL DU MONTE	NIKON FA	24 MM	1/60	F32
52	HOW STEAN GORGE	NIKON FA	24 MM	1/15	F22
53	GRASSINGTON	NIKON FA	50 MM	1/60	F16
54	SHEEP	NIKON FA	50 MM	1/500	F16
55	KILNSEY CRAG	NIKON FA	24 MM	1/125	F22
56	ARNCLIFFE, YORKSHIRE DALES	NIKON FA	50 MM	1/250	F11
57	GORDALE SCAR	BRONICA S2A	75 MM	1/15	F22
58	MALHAM COVE	NIKON FA	24 MM	1/60	F16
59	SEMERWATER	NIKON FA	24 MM	1/15	F22
60	AYSGARTH FALLS	NIKON FA	50 MM	1/60	F11
61	OLD GANG MINES	NIKON FA	50 MM	1/125	F16
62	RICHMOND	NIKON FA	24 MM	1/30	F32
63	GUNNERSIDE	NIKON FA	50 MM	1/125	F16
64	WINDOW AND WALL, HIGH DALES	NIKON FA	50 MM	1/30	F11
65	DALES FARM SCENE	NIKON FA	24 MM	1/250	F16
66	BUTTERTUBS PASS	NIKON FA	24 MM	1/15	F32
67	HARDRAW FORCE	BRONICA S2A	75 MM	60 SECS	F16
68	RIBBLEHEAD VIADUCT	NIKON FA	50 MM	1/125	F8
69	BELOW INGLEBOROUGH	NIKON FA	24 MM	1/8	F32
70	PENDRAGON	NIKON FA	100 MM	1/250	F11

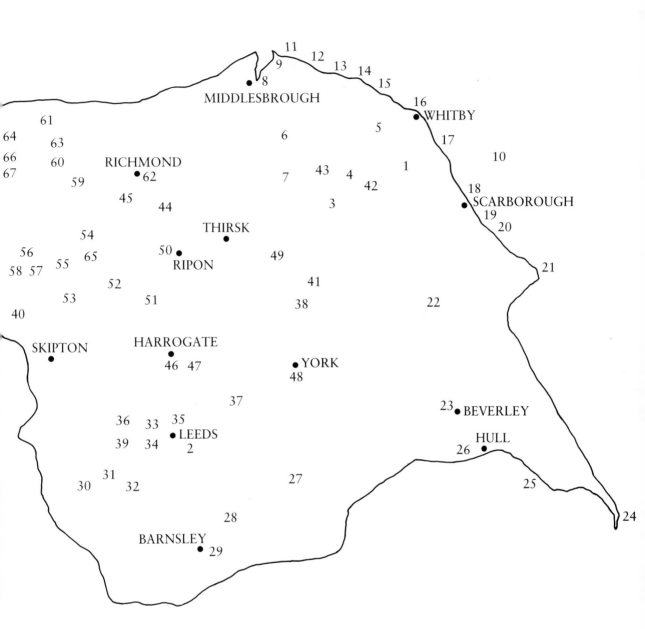

11
9 12
8 13 14
MIDDLESBROUGH 15
16
WHITBY
61 5
64 17
63 6 10
66 60
67 RICHMOND
59 62 7 43 4 1
45 42 18
44 3 SCARBOROUGH
19
THIRSK 20
54
56 50
58 57 55 65 RIPON 49 21
52 41
53 51 38 22
40
HARROGATE
SKIPTON 46 47 YORK
48
37
23 BEVERLEY
36 33 35
39 34 LEEDS HULL
2 26
31 27 25
30 32 24
28
BARNSLEY
29

144

PHOTOGRAPHERS' BRITAIN